GET REAL!

GET REAL!

MAL FLETCHER

WORD PUBLISHING

Nelson Word Ltd
Milton Keynes, England

WORD AUSTRALIA
Kilsyth, Victoria, Australia

WORD COMMUNICATIONS LTD
Vancouver, B.C., Canada

STRUIK CHRISTIAN BOOKS (PTY) LTD
Maitland, South Africa

JOINT DISTRIBUTORS SINGAPORE –
ALBY COMMERCIAL ENTERPRISES PTE LTD
and
CAMPUS CRUSADE

CHRISTIAN MARKETING NEW ZEALAND LTD
Havelock North, New Zealand

JENSCO LTD
Hong Kong

SALVATION BOOK CENTRE
Malaysia

GET REAL!

Published by Nelson Word Ltd., Milton Keynes, 1993.

ISBN 0-85009-594-8   (Australia ISBN 1-86258-251-3)

Unless otherwise indicated, Scripture quotations are from The Youth
Bible, New Century Version, copyright © 1991 by Word Publishing,
Dallas, Texas 75039. Used by permission.

Other Scripture quotations are from the following sources:
    The King James Version (KJV).
    The New American Standard Bible (NASB), © 1960, 1962,
    1963, 1968, 1971, 1972, 1973, 1975, 1977 by the Lockman
    Foundation.
    The New International Version (NIV), copyright © 1973, 1978,
    1984 by International Bible Society.

Permission applied for to use the quotations accredited in the
footnotes.

Reproduced, printed and bound in Great Britain for Nelson Word
Ltd. by Cox and Wyman Ltd., Reading.

93 94 95 96 / 10 9 8 7 6 5 4 3 2 1

Contents

Acknowledgements

I'm always aware that most worthwhile achievements in life come about as the result of team work. With that in mind, I'd like to express my thanks to the other members of this 'team':

To Noël Halsey and all at Nelson Word—for taking risks and seeing the importance of ministry to young leaders.

To Stan and Norm Moulton at Word (Australia)—for believing in me.

To my colleagues in Youth Alive—for making the gospel understandable to the young.

To my able itinerary manager, Christy McClay—for personal support and devotion to the cause.

To my parents and extended family—for constant encouragement.

To my children, Deanna, Grant and Jade—for being the best kids in all the world!

To my patient and wonderful wife Davina—for always being there when the crowds go home (and on my bad days). You're the best and I love you.

To the Lord—He knows what He's done for me!

Introduction

Why Should I Calm Down?!

Have you ever seen a dog climbing Mount Everest for the kicks? How about a fun-crazy cat parachuting from a plane at twenty thousand feet? Or a horse bungee-jumping? How about a very fit chicken running for Olympic glory? No?

Few people have, and there's a very good reason for this: only human beings are built for heroism. Oh sure, Lassie is one notable exception, but by and large we *Homo sapiens* have cornered the market on adventurism. Every one of us wants to achieve something memorable and significant.

Ernest Becker won the Pulitzer Prize for reminding us of this fact. In his book *Denial of Death* Becker said that our greatest fear is the fear of death. We're afraid, he wrote, because we cannot bear the idea that we may be forgotten, that things will go on without us. So we try all our lives to achieve something which will give us a certain kind of immortality.

No one, given the chance, would like to turn up at their own funeral and hear their best friends saying things like: 'Now, what was his name again?' and 'Can someone just remind me what it was I liked about her?'

I remember my first *Rocky* film. I stared up in awe at the larger-than-life story unfolding above me on the big screen. As the heroic saga reached its climax, I was suddenly aware that there was one difference between myself and every other person in that cinema. They were watching Sylvester Stallone play Rocky Balboa, but all I could see was *me* up there trading blows with Mr T. I was a legend in my own mind. We all possess a heroism drive.

Have you ever been to a concert and found yourself daydreaming about being up on stage yourself? Did you ever pick up a trusty tennis racket and play along with your favourite band on the radio? That's all part of wanting to be significant.

I love working with young people, for one reason in particular—they are more honest than many of their elders. They know they're built for heroism and they go and grab it with both hands, and feet. Older people tend to hide their youthful dreams under a cloak of respectability, for fear of risking anything or rocking the social or economic security boat.

Young people love a challenge and a risk. Sadly, the church has not always seen this. Preachers have often called the young to: 'Come to Jesus and calm down.'

A couple of years ago I saw a road sign which I think summed up this distorted view of Christianity. Sometimes you see signs which say things like, 'Quiet please, hospital' or 'Silence please, home for the aged'. This one said, 'Quiet please, church'. Now that's *really* going to get people interested in Christianity!

What is that sign saying about us? If you give your life to Jesus you'll lose your edge, you'll slow to a walk, you'll get respectability.

Nothing could be farther from the heart of Jesus

Christ! He calls us to *upset* the status quo—to challenge the way things are whenever the way things are meets with God's disapproval. He commands us to rebel, just as He did. He was not afraid of controversy or rejection, choosing to tell the truth even when it would cost Him His life.

Now, there is something dignifying in becoming a Christian. You realise for the first time that you are not a monkey who got lucky! A wise and rational God made you for a great purpose. But dignity and respectability are two different things. To be a friend of the world, to concern yourself with being socially acceptable above all else is, according to the Bible, to set yourself up as an enemy of God (Jas. 4:4).

My grandfather is 87 years of age. He's the oldest surviving member of his church. He has a five-inch parting through the middle of his hair (his hair went to heaven before he did). He came to me not too long ago and, pointing to his bald spot, said, 'You see that, son? You know where I got that, son? Rap dancing, that's where!'

I could just see my grandpa's head spinning across the polished floor in the foyer of his church. He has more fun in him than many 25-year-olds I meet. He has refused to 'calm down'. I can't see Jesus, the greatest rebel in history, turning up at a 1990s youth rally and calling people to 'calm down a bit . . . '!

Jesus said we are to preach the Kingdom of God, which is most often a very different kingdom to the one we see around us (Matt. 24:14). And we're not only to talk about it, but to live in a way which will demonstrate the Kingdom way of life in practical situations. We are born again to enter into the Kingdom (John 3:3) and to have it enter into us (Luke 17:21). Then we must let the Kingdom within us escape and affect every part of our lives (Phil. 2:12).

At least one Old Testament prophet, pointing to the advent of the Kingdom when Messiah appeared, told of God's intention to raise up a prophetic generation of young men and women (Joel 2:28–29). The prophetic voice is the one which sometimes cries alone in the wilderness, 'Prepare the way for the Lord' (Matt. 3:3). It is the voice of the holy rebel calling for God's justice and compassion. It challenges what is there and points the way to something higher and greater.

Such was the call of Jeremiah, himself a young man when he became a rebel with a cause. 'Today I have put you in charge of nations and kingdoms,' God said. 'You will pull up and tear down . . . build up and plant' (Jer. 1:10).

Martin Luther King had a similar understanding of what it is to call for change by the way we live. He had a dream, he said, of an America in which people were not judged by the colour of their skin, but by the quality of their character. To achieve this he knew that Americans would need to 'tear down' some of their existing practices and 'build up' more godly patterns in their place.

So Jesus calls us to rebel. But His brand of rebellion has nothing to do with the arrogant independence and unsubmissive attitudes which Scripture condemns. It is a radical commitment to live my life as Jesus would if He were in my Reeboks.

Too many Christians pray 'Thy Kingdom come' while they harbour secret hopes that nothing will really change. Why should we want God's Kingdom when the one we live in is quite comfortable, thank you very much?

According to Dr J. I. Packer, one of the reasons many modern Christians don't talk openly about the Lord's second coming, and even find it an 'embarrassing' subject, is that: 'This is a time of worldly-mindedness, at least among the prosperous Christians of the West. We think less and less about the better things that Christ will bring us at His appearance, because our thoughts are increasingly absorbed by the good things we enjoy here.'[1]

This book is not for people who are satisfied with what they have here and now. It is for those who will say with one rock band, 'I still haven't found what I'm looking for.' It's for young people—and young-thinking people—who want to live prophetically. This book was written for those heroic hearts who want to learn how to rebel. It is for people who know God has called them to leadership and are asking, 'What now?'

Today, the true voice of God's Spirit comes to afflict the comfortable and comfort the afflicted. If you're listening for that radical call read on and, whatever you do, don't calm down!

Announce this among the nations:
  Prepare for war!
Wake up the soldiers! . . .
Lord, send your soldiers
  to gather the nations (Joel 3:9,11).

---

1. J. I. Packer, *I Want to Be a Christian* (Kingsway, 1985), p. 59.

1

Vision: Power to Change the World

If you were God and you wanted to change the world for ever, you'd hardly set out to do it through an obscure itinerant preacher who only twice or three times travelled more than 30 miles from his home, a small village of around 500 inhabitants. You'd hardly want your world-changer to spend all his lifetime in an insignificant country which measured just 126 miles north to south and 46 west to east. But then, you're not God, are you? All of this was part of the Vision. No one can change the world like a visionary. A visionary can build a lot from very little.

It's a chilly December morning in Bucharest. The downtrodden people of Romania have listened to another self-congratulatory speech by their tyrannical leader. This time, however, there's a startling difference in their response. Ceausescu, speaking from his favourite balcony overlooking Palace Square, is shocked to hear members of the crowd jeering him with the chant: 'Ceausescu Dictatorul'—Ceausescu Dictator.

Just two days later, students march downtown in a

show of defiance and hatred for the autocrat. He sends tanks out to greet them. Rather than fire on the crowds, however, the tank crews are shooting into the air. Army commanders, like almost everyone else in the country, have had enough of Ceausescu and his domineering wife. The growing crowds then set their sights on the Central Committee building, the home of Communist rule. Ceausescu, by now painfully aware that he can no longer hold on to power, takes a brief helicopter ride into history.

Shortly after these events, news of the revolution has spread far and wide and the country is breathing a huge sigh of relief—a relief mixed with apprehension, as the much-feared secret police have gone underground and may strike back at any time. International journalists are eagerly making their way into the capital, desperate to give the world a taste of Eastern Europe's newest revolution.

One award-winning reporter later recalls his own entry on the scene: 'We had arrived on a small charter flight. The airport was dark . . . We flagged down a man who drove us into town in his sedan. I asked what was happening. "Oh," he said, "just a small revolution in a small place." '[1]

Just a small revolution in a small place—but the world took notice and the Communist regimes of other lands began to sense that their time too was running out. In a nation where ordinary citizens were as harassed and maligned as they were in Romania, in a land where paranoia ruled the rulers—every typewriter in the country was registered with the secret police—it was vision in human

---

1. David and Peter Turnley and Mort Rosenblum, *Moments of Revolution* (Stewart, Tabori & Chang, 1990), pp. 24–26.

hearts which kept the fires of revolution alight. In the end, it was university students, Romania's young leaders, who decided they would hide their vision no longer. They were the first to take to the streets, they were the ones to inspire the dreams of others.

Vision is a very powerful force. Someone has said, 'Faith is the daring of the soul to go farther than it can see.' But it's only hopeful hearts that dare to dream and reach out in faith. It's hard to plan for a positive future if you don't think there's going to be one. Scripture says that faith is 'being sure of the things we hope for' (Heb. 11:1). Vision is born out of hope, which is why Christians must fight the widespread insurgence of despair in the youth culture of today.

Faith is the Bible's word for hope in action. Without hope, there can be no vision and without vision there can be no faith action. Without action born out of faith, it is impossible to please God (Heb. 11:6).

Vision is the nourishment of revolutionaries. It motivates us and drives us forward to better things. In secondary school, one young guy thought he might like to be a priest. He worked towards that end for a time but finally decided it wasn't for him—besides, he liked girls too much. Still a teenager, he thought he'd try his hand at wrestling. After all, he was the athletic type. Sadly, however, some bones were busted and so was his dream of becoming another Hulk Hogan. Then he turned his hand to acting. He acted in the usual school plays and, when he left school, he took acting lessons.

In between his classes he waited on tables at a restaurant and acted in small plays in his spare time. He got some bit parts in totally forgettable films, but persisted and eventually became a hit. His name: Tom Cruise. He's made himself quite a name on the big screen and he's paid a lot better than your friendly neighbourhood priest. But he wasn't born into this success—he worked towards it, following one dream after another until he found what he was good at. Tom's dreams may have changed, but his determination to have a dream did not.

Vision moves us forward to each new stage of life. Robert Schuller is right when he says that dreams not only help us to success, they keep us alive.

One granny from Oregon lost her ability to dream. The doctors diagnosed her as having Alzheimer's disease, a debilitating condition which slowly erodes a person's mental powers. Still, the doctors said, their diagnosis might be wrong—and even if it weren't she should still enjoy several more productive and rich years. But Mrs Adkins did not want to go on. With her husband's approval, she flew to Detroit to meet a pathologist who had gained some notoriety for his invention of a 'suicide machine'.

One Monday evening, while her husband waited in a nearby hotel, Mrs Adkins lay down in the back of the doctor's Volkswagen van and was hooked up to the home-made contraption. Minutes later she injected a sedative into her system followed by a deadly dose of potassium chloride. She had been fit enough to beat her grown son at tennis just the week before, but this woman saw no positive vision for her future.

Vision motivates us. Vision keeps us from despair and defeatism. But it is important for yet another reason. It keeps us on the right track in our walk with God. I have a small collection of advertisements taken from Christian magazines. I read them every so often to jolt myself into reality. One of my favourites reads like this:

CHRISTIAN CAP LIGHTS: Not Just Another Cap! Christian Cap Lights are a baseball-style cap with a powerful halogen lamp built into the visor. You can see 6 feet in front wherever you look—HANDS FREE! Christian Cap Lights are great for reading, writing, working . . . any place you need a light, the small inconspicuous lamp is not noticeable until you turn it on and delight your friends! Special Price: $17:95!

Here's another:

Flat tyre . . . Out of petrol . . . Car broken down . . . A loved one is ill . . . You're lost . . . STRANDED! It happens to all of us sooner or later. You need help! Will anybody stop? Who can you trust? You hear such terrible stories!

A brother or sister in Christ—YOU CAN TRUST A BROTHER OR SISTER IN CHRIST! But you must let them know you need help. You need the CHRIS-TIANS' ROADSIDE ALERT to proclaim a Christian in need.

The CHRISTIANS' ROADSIDE ALERT is a two-foot tall, double-sided sign made of highly visible safety-yellow plastic. It is lightweight and folds flat for easy storage in even the smallest car boot—until you need it. Be prepared the next time it happens to you! Put one in every car! $19.95.

Somehow I can't see Jesus or the apostles flogging Christian Caplights or Roadside Alerts! These advertisements and others like them would be funny if they weren't so serious. It seems to me that some sections of the church have lost the plot somewhere—some of us have forgotten what we're here for. We need a new infusion of vision.

You can learn a lot from reading greeting cards. Here's one card quote I like: 'Youth is not a time of life . . . Nobody grows old merely by living a number of years. People grow old by deserting their ideals.' Have some churches not lost their vitality, their punch, because they have lost their ideals, and abandoned their pursuit of vision?

Seeing Starts with Looking . . .

Okay, so vision is vital to being a leader, to life itself. But how do I catch hold of God's vision for me and for those I lead? How do I know whether the dreams I have are God's dreams for me?

Joe Christian is taking a shower. He loves his time in the shower because it gives him a chance to 'wash and pray'. Today he's absent-mindedly mouthing a prayer he's said a thousand times: 'Lord, show me your will for my life . . . ' He says it, then thinks no more about it.

Suddenly, a humungous Belshazarrian hand (à la Daniel chapter 5) punches a huge hole in the bathroom window. The index finger begins to scrawl on the steamed-up wall tiles. It's writing something in laser print. He recoils in horror, chewing on the soap-on-a-rope. He knows what this is—the finger of God, and it's writing God's plan for his life right there on the wall. When the steam clears the hand is nowhere to be seen, but two words are glaring at him from across the room. So this is God's plan for my life, he thinks. 'Just two words,' he laments, 'is that all there is? I want my offerings back!'

The two words are: 'DO SOMETHING!'

I have three children. I know that, come the school holidays, they will more than likely change from resourceful, imaginative kids into bored, brain-dead jellyfish. They will come to their mother or me with the same old complaint every second day: 'I've got nothing to do . . . '

What do we say in reply? '*Find* something . . . ' And that's just what the Lord says to His kids at times: 'Stop asking for guidance. Just get out there and *do* something. The rest will fall into place.'

Have you ever tried to steer a stationary car? It's a great way to get a hernia! But once you get the car moving, even just a little, it's easy to steer the car in the right direction. God is waiting for His people to take responsibility and get involved in someone's need so that He can steer them into His plan.

God is searching the earth for people who can make decisions for themselves based on the opportunities around them now. Some sage has remarked that, 'Between tomorrow's dream and yesterday's regret is today's opportunity.' People who seize opportunities become God's visionaries.

Mother Theresa has taught that, 'Jesus comes thinly disguised in the poor of the world.' Tony Campolo has put it this way: 'Jesus waits behind every person in need, waiting to be served by us.' And Martin Luther King made this observation: 'Life's most urgent and persistent question is this—what are you doing for others?'

Something is wrong. We go to church where we will pray, 'Lord, show me your will for my life.' To get there we will pass hospitals filled with lonely people, prisons bursting at the seams with forgotten and angry men, homes where single mums battle to hold a family together and others where the cries of the kids can't be heard over the screams of their parents. Why don't we stop long enough to find the will of God at the side of the road?

Melbourne's Pentridge prison, one of the largest and oldest in Australia, is no holiday resort. I've never been a resident there—thank God—but I have visited several times. One occasion really stands out in my memory.

I was called upon to visit a young man I'd known since childhood. He was little more than a toddler when my mother and father began to take him on our annual family holidays. He'd come from a broken home and, as the years went by, he and his younger brother became honorary members of the family. Our country holidays helped to get them out of the city for a while.

I thought about those holidays as I watched Kevin from behind a half-inch thick glass partition in the remand section of Pentridge. He hadn't even been brought to trial yet and was already forced to live in one of the most squalid areas in the prison. With real remorse he told me, via an ancient two-way intercom system, how he'd come to this place. His live-in girlfriend had given birth to his son and then, after they'd been living together for a year or so, she left him for another boyfriend. It came as a real shock to him and he couldn't control his frustration. Like a great many young men, Kevin felt he had no one to turn to. In anger he resorted to physical violence—he called on his ex-girlfriend, assaulted the other man and took the child.

So here he was on charges of assault and kidnap. He wept as he told me he'd rather die than spend much more time in 'this hole'.

Two things stayed with me as I left the prison that day. One was Kevin's brokenness. Here was a strapping young Aussie male sobbing and grieving like a child. The other thing which shook me was just how restricted he was in his movements. He'd described for me an average day in jail which included fifteen hours locked in a cramped cell. There was no more freedom to do as he pleased—he marched to someone else's drum. I was shaken when I left prison that day.

I thought of Kevin when, a short time later, I was studying something Paul said in 2 Corinthians 5:14. Here he's telling the often hardhearted Corinthians just why he keeps giving heart and soul to help them. 'The love of Christ constraineth us,' he says, 'because we thus judge, that one died for all . . . ' (KJV). The word we read as 'constraineth' in the King James Version is actually a word which means to 'arrest as a prisoner'. The love of Christ arrested Paul so that he couldn't help but get involved. Like Kevin, Paul suffered the brokenness of imprisonment and the restriction of freedom which it brought. He found himself bound to help, arrested by the love of Christ.

That's the kind of passion it would take if we're to see nations really affected by the Good News. As Larry Crabb has it, 'The church has lost its power because it loves so poorly.'[2]

Each of us was built to change our world in some way—to rebel against the status quo which, because we live in a fallen world, is always falling short of God's ideal. We were all created to be heroes. The power to change our world does not come to the strong, though. It comes to the weak, the dependent and the vulnerable: the 'poor in spirit' (Matt. 5:3 KJV). This power comes not from above, from higher earthly potentates, but from below, from

2. Larry Crabb, *Inside Out* (NavPress, 1988), p. 98.

people who allow us to influence them because they know we love them. The power to revolutionise our age comes not through domination, exploitation and tyranny, but through service. It is not the power of the sword but the power of the towel.

> Imagine Jesus, biceps bulging beneath a seamless robe with flowing cape, reclining at supper with His disciples. The forces of evil have been collecting for months and are about to kill him, but don't worry, all the power ever created is coursing through His body. He gets up—this man surrounded by overwhelming evil forces—walks over to the disciples and with all this incredible power . . . begins to do what? 'He got up from the meal, took off his outer clothing, and wrapped a towel around his waist. After that, he poured water into a basin and began to wash his disciples' feet . . . ' So that is what he does with power! He washes feet.[3]

Are You for Real?

Early in Australia's history the Anglican archbishop of Sydney developed a real concern for the horsemen, the 'bushies', who lived in what are now the western suburbs of the city. He called in one of his most gifted preachers. 'Go and start a mission among the bushmen,' he told the eager priest. 'Do whatever you need to do. You've got my full support.'

Delighted to be asked by the archbishop himself, the

---

3. Gayle Erwin, *The Jesus Style* (Word Books, 1983), p. 146.

preacher rode out to meet his new parishioners. To his surprise word had got around that he was coming and a posse had been sent out to meet him just outside the settlement.

The tall, bronzed leader of the pack, a real Marlboro man, angled his horse up to the preacher's and said: 'Look mate, we've come out to tell you we don't want your kind out here. We've got no time for the church—it's never done anything for us. Frankly, we'll be an embarrassment to you and you to us. So tell your archbishop that we're not interested in religion.'

Deflated and upset, the priest rode back to town and made his unhappy report to the church authorities. The archbishop was heartbroken. He really thought he'd heard from God on this one. Then he learned something which made his day. A young man had recently graduated from seminary—a man who was once a prize fighter. Now the archbishop *knew* he'd heard the call of God!

'Go west young man,' the new recruit was told. So off he went on his first assignment for the church, full of enthusiasm. Again the welcoming committee rode out to greet him. They told him to go home and forget them. But he stood his ground. So they suggested a little deal might be made.

'I tell you what we'll do,' said the head of the group. 'I'll get down off my horse, all my mates will get off theirs, then you fight us one at a time, man-to-man. If you're still standing at the end we'll let you come and live with us. If you're not, we'll send the pieces home!'

The big Christian thought for a moment and then climbed down from his steed, like an Aussie John Wayne. 'Sounds fair to me,' he smiled. As he rolled up his sleeves he said, 'Of course you know this isn't the way the church normally does business. But, well, who's first?'

The bushmen laughed. Their leader strolled over to the preacher and clapped him on the back. 'You don't really need to do that, mate,' he grinned. 'We just wanted to know if you were for real.'

I think we need a few more Anglican boxers in the church today, don't you?

Where Do I Start?

OK, you say, I want to get involved with the needs of others. I want to find vision as I reach out. But how do I know where to start? I mean, the world's such a big place. I can't solve all its problems. Where do I channel my efforts and energies? What are my gifts? After all, as one writer has put it, 'There is no "self-made" successful man or woman. There are only people smart enough or grateful enough to be good stewards of their gifts.'[4]

Some people who really want to stall for time use this question as a smoke screen. They want to spend six weeks doing a Bible study on gifts, yet when the series is over they'll be as selfish as ever. But that's not always the case. There is a genuine need in all of us to find out what our potential is, to discover where we can be most effective. How do I find out?

First of all, stop looking for your gifts and start looking at your motivations. Every one of us is motivated about something. It might be sport, music, studying, befriending the lonely, encouraging those with terminal blues or being a leader of others—the list goes on. What

---

4. Quoted by Ron Boehme, *Leadership for the Twentieth Century* (Frontline Communications, 1989), p. 97.

gets you excited? What keeps you awake at night? What makes you angry about the world around you? What do you want to fight for? Here are six broad types of motivation. Check which of these might apply to you. When you know what motivates you, you've uncovered a strong clue as to where your God-given gifts are:

1. Relational motivations: Some of us are particularly gifted in social areas, in dealing with people one-to-one or in groups. This kind of motivation is vital if you hope to be a leader. In the New Testament, Barnabas used his relational gifts to bring Saul of Tarsus into favour with the apostles and thus get him started in ministry (Acts 9:26–27).

2. Intellectual motivations: There are people in every group who appear to be 'brighter' than the rest. If that's you, don't apologise for being intelligent. Recognise it as a strength God can use. Apollos, the great teacher spoken of in Acts, was a 'learned man, with a thorough knowledge of the Scriptures' (Acts 18:24 NIV).

3. Mechanical motivations: Thank God not every Christian is called to be a full-time public speaker! After all, if there were no motor mechanics out there I'd be in big trouble. Carpenters may be as called to their vocation as pastors and evangelists are to theirs. What can God do with a carpenter? Read the gospels! Paul was a tentmaker who sometimes used his gift to support himself while he started churches.

4. Artistic motivations: The arts are alive and well in many churches! Creative believers are learning not to stifle their talent or take it elsewhere for expression. For too long we have allowed the secular world to set the tone and corner the market for artistic expression. During the Renaissance, if you were a master who wanted to show your *pièce de résistance*, you painted it in a chapel or cathedral. In modern times Christians have largely kept out of the world of art, perhaps afraid that they cannot compete or have nothing to say. In Bible times, Solomon was one man who employed artistic abilities to tell his generation about the nature of God through proverbs, architecture and songs.

5. Athletic motivations: It may seem odd to say that God can use athletic giftings, but he can. One of my favourite films of all time is the modern classic *Chariots of Fire* which traces the development of two British Olympians as they prepare for the 1924 games. One of them, Eric Liddell, was a committed Christian runner who held his faith in God above his preoccupation with sport. He made front-page news by refusing to compete in the 100-metre dash—his speciality—because it was run on a Sunday. He later ran in the 400-metre race instead and stunned the world again—by winning!

He has a great line in the film. His sister is telling him that he has no right to run. He's called to be a missionary, she claims, and shouldn't be wasting his time on sport. His reply is one which should encourage every Christian who excels at sport: 'Jenny, when God made me, He made me fast and when I run I feel His pleasure.' In real life Liddell did go on to become a missionary, but not until he'd brought glory to God on the Olympic sports field.

If Israel's King David were alive today, he wouldn't

need steroids to compete with the world's best. Who else but an athletic man could have slain Goliath and fought so skilfully in so many battles?

6. Spiritual motivations: It seems to me that, for whatever reason, some people are more spiritually attuned or sensitive than others. Perhaps it's just that they've made a stronger commitment to walking in the Spirit and putting aside the flesh. Elisha was a man with very definite spiritual motivations and a real inner strength. Perhaps that's why God told Elijah to appoint Elisha as his successor.

It is true, of course, that we are all gifted or motivated in more than one of these areas. There is no rule which says, for example, that a gifted athlete can't also be a spiritual giant. The point is that our concept of giftings is too narrow.

When my dad was growing up in church his generation were led to believe that if you couldn't preach, or lead worship, or run some department of the church, you didn't have a ministry. 'Gifted' was a word which was only applied to people who fulfilled a public role in church leadership. The church can and must encourage people to achieve excellence for God's glory wherever they are most talented. We must all learn how to submit our motivations to the Holy Spirit so that they serve His purposes and not ours. Look at what you're good at and start using that skill to share the Lord with others. That's where vision begins.

Hearing is Believing . . .

If you'd known Shah Jahan you would have invited him to all your parties. He was a winner. Everyone wanted to know him. He was a Mogul emperor. He had money, fame, power and the love of a beautiful woman who became his wife.

Jahan was not a pretty picture when his wife died. He just couldn't get over it. He was so upset that he vowed to build a huge billion-dollar temple in honour of her memory. At first he thought of doing things the predictable way: building the edifice then placing her poor dead body within. Then he thought, no, I'll go one better than that. He set about building the temple around the coffin.

He found the land he wanted to use and placed the wooden casket in the centre of the open field. Plans were drawn up and the work began. Jahan slowly began to come out of his depression and showed signs of actually enjoying this new project. Soon he was completely engrossed in the whole thing. It was going to be one of the wonders of the world and a fitting tribute to his own abilities and influence.

One day, as he surveyed the work, he stubbed his royal toe on an old wooden box which had become half buried in the builders' rubble. In pain, he ordered that the box be removed and thrown away. It was only later that he realised what he'd done—his wife was in that box!

Shah Jahan did something he was good at, but he forgot the plot along the way. His gifts consumed him and he lost sight of what it was all for. Unless we keep our spiritual ears open, all our good efforts and intentions can actually lead us away from God's vision for us. In all of our planning and dreaming, we need to hear from God so that we avoid building what looks good to us rather than what suits His purposes.

It's not easy to answer the question, 'How do I get a

word from God?' mainly because when God speaks, He speaks to the intuitive part of a person—the spiritual, intangible dimension of the heart. Our dialogue with God can be difficult to describe or analyse. The Bible is our only source of reliable information on how this happens, and there are some key principles we need to lay hold of if we're going to hear God's direction in the midst of our labours:

Waiting on God

I bought a radio once. It was an awesome piece of hi-tech wizardry. It had slide controls for this and knobs for that. The salesman told me it was the hottest model available—the sounds I'd hear would be unbelievable. So I took it home and eagerly pulled it from its box. I was ready to get down!

I switched it on and waited for the magic to begin. To my dismay, all that emanated from the speakers was a monotonous humming sound. No rhythm, no beat, just humming. I took it back to the store and demanded a refund. The salesman asked if I'd tuned it in to the right station. I was confused. 'What do you mean "tune it in"?' I asked. 'I thought you just had to turn it on and it did the rest for you!'

When it comes to laying hold of a vision for our lives, we need to tune in to God's wavelength so that we're not listening to AM while he's playing on FM. I think the Lord probably talks to us more often than we realise—we just haven't taken time to tune in.

Tuning in is what the Bible calls 'waiting on God' or 'seeking God's face' or 'finding rest in God'. These terms are used often in the Bible, so this is an important principle (see Ps. 130:5; 62:5; Isa. 8:17).

The single greatest characteristic of waiting on God is the constant discipline it requires (see Mark 1:35; Ps. 25:5; 55:17). Part of the discipline of waiting on God is regular reading of the Bible. Note the words 'regular' and 'reading'. Sometimes we read the Bible only very occasionally and we wonder why our antennae aren't working too well. Then, because we feel guilty, we try to make up for our lack of discipline by doing marathon study sessions with a dictionary and a concordance.

In those sessions, we try to find hidden meanings in every word of the Bible and we make things too complicated for ourselves. The Bible is not a theology textbook or a series of clever essays on difficult subjects. It's a book about life—life with our fellow man and life with our God. If you stop to dissect every word, you often miss the overall picture of what the Lord is saying. Real revelation comes more often out of short regular readings than guilt-induced endurance rallies!

In-depth Bible study is a very good discipline, but it cannot replace regular readings. The Bible needs to be a habit.

Waiting on God involves prayerful, systematic reading of the Bible—taking one book at a time, not jumping from one to another with no rhyme or reason. It also involves learning to meditate on what you're reading. Phil Pringle teaches that meditation is the 'digestive faculty of the soul'.[5] He writes that:

> Christian meditation is not like Eastern meditation where people empty their minds. This is entirely different. To meditate is to mutter

5. Phil Pringle, *Faith* (Seam of Gold, 1991), p. 82.

the word of God to ourselves . . . to repeat it
to yourself again and again. Like a cow
chewing its cud . . . As we speak and hear the
word of God our faith continually grows.[6]

If you're a leader, you might find yourself building
sermons as you read and meditate. Some say that this is
wrong—and, if taken to extremes, it can prevent us hearing
from God for ourselves. But looking for sermons isn't so
bad if you're willing to live them before you preach them!

Receiving God's word

God will speak, in His time, to a heart that is inclined to
hear (see Ps. 140:1–8; Hab 2:3). Of course, His time-
frame and ours will not always coincide. (God doesn't use
a calendar or year planner.) The initiative is always His.
We may need to stay in prayer for weeks or months before
we hear God's word of vision, but when it comes it must
find a heart ready to obey (and hands which are already
active).

Ali Hafed was a happy farmer until one day
someone told him about the wealth to be found in
diamonds. He asked where diamonds might be found and
was told to look for a white stream which flowed through
white sands surrounded by high mountains. There it was
said he would find diamonds.

He sold his farm, left his family in the care of a
neighbour and set out on his quest. He travelled throughout the Middle East, but sadly found no diamonds. He
finally came one day to the coast of Spain, penniless. In
despair he threw himself into the sea and drowned.

6. Ibid.

Meanwhile, the man who bought his farm happened to spot a black chunk of rock as he watered his camel one day. He took it home, and soon afterwards was showing it to a visitor who excitedly informed him that he'd found a diamond. Actually, he'd discovered a diamond mine. It became one of the most famous in the world, from which one of the crown jewels of England was taken. Ali Hafed should have stuck around.[7]

Sometimes you need to be in the right place at the right time. What is it that keeps us where God's vision can find us? Patience.

Patience is the surrendering of control. Do you know why people worry about things? Because ever since the fall of humanity, we've been trying to win control over our own destinies. We struggle and strive to call the shots. When things happen which we didn't foresee, we complain about what a rotten world this is. It's because we feel unable to make changes in the real world that we make 'pretend' ones in the unreal area of the imagination. Worry is our way of playing with all the possibilities and changing outcomes in our heads. Worry is surrogate control. It is grown-ups playing pretend.

Patience involves being yielded—giving up the right to pull the strings either through physical effort or mental worry. 'Being patient,' says Pringle, 'keeps us behind God.'[8] It stops us from walking out of step with Him and trying to rush ahead. It prevents us from being in the wrong place at the wrong time when God's call arrives!

If you're in a hurry to change the world, count to ten and think again.

---

7. Robert Schuller, *Discover Your Possibilities* (Harvest House, 1978), pp. 150–151.

8. Pringle, op. cit. p. 107.

Bringing a strategy to God

This is where many could-be visionaries fall down and miss their piece of the action. I was speaking at a conference in England and opened up with the statement: 'A visionary is the third most dangerous thing to the kingdom of darkness.' This seemed to surprise some, who perhaps thought a visionary should be number one threat to Satan! I went on: 'The second most dangerous thing to the devil is a visionary with a strategy.' A few nods of approval here. 'The *most* dangerous thing to Satan's kingdom is a visionary who has a strategy and is involved in activity.'

Without strategy, visions are just that—things seen from a distance, castles in the air. Castles in the air are great until you step out the door!

A pastor friend of mine says that, 'Vision without work is just dreaming; work without vision is just drudgery.' With strategy, visions have a way of becoming reality and plans can be translated into activity. That's when visionaries become dangerous— when they start doing things with their dreams.

Have you ever wondered why God gave us brains? I mean, so few of us seem willing to use them. I never had a good teacher in school who didn't expect me to do homework. I complained about some of it at the time, but with hindsight I can see that the things I remember best are those I spent most time discovering for myself.

Being the Great Teacher that He is, I can't see God not giving us homework in the classroom of vision. I've found that once He has begun to speak to you on a thing, He will require you to do some follow-up for yourself. He won't tell you everything about how to achieve His vision—you'll have to fill in some of the blanks for yourself.

Let's say, for example, you feel God is leading you into a ministry of youth counselling. God might very well leave you to make investigations about what kind of counselling is needed by kids in your area—careers guidance, family conflict counselling, sexual counselling, etc. He might want you to find out what kinds of personnel you'll need to get the vision happening. You might then need to think about where the money's coming from.

In every Godly dream, there is His part and our part. He may suggest the vision; I may have to suggest the strategy.

Wait on God ... again ... and again
OK, so you've done some homework. You've begun to shape a concrete strategy. You're ready to go ... Let me at 'em, you say.

Hold on a bit! Homework needs to be corrected by the Teacher. Otherwise, how will you know if you've made a mistake?

Even when I think I've heard from God on a matter, even when I've then checked out the options and formed a strategy, I will need to wait upon His approval for my scheme. He must have the right to change the plan, or reject it altogether.

Waiting on God is the key to wisdom. Excessive haste will kill a good dream before it's born.

Paul the apostle knew the benefit of waiting on God. This waiting wasn't a passive thing where he just sat around hoping something would come up for him to do. He was active all the time: dreaming, planning, travelling and preaching. Yet he had learned the discipline of tuning his ear daily to hear from God.

There are two occasions recorded in Acts where Paul actually set out to enter a certain place and the Lord wouldn't let him (Acts 16:7). Paul was able to work at a feverish pace and still wait on God for final approval on all his plans! He was sensitive enough to know the voice of the Spirit and humble enough to change his plans accordingly.

In the midst of our planning and working, we must keep listening for the Boss's voice. Once we feel a sense of peace about a plan, or at least the absence of a 'stop' signal, we can proceed knowing that the Lord will watch over His word to perform it (Jer. 1:2).

Fatal Distractions!

Nehemiah was a man of great vision. While in exile from Jerusalem, the Lord gave him a dream and a call—he was to return to Israel and rebuild the walls of its capital. It was an exciting but daunting task, one for which he would need all the wisdom and courage he could muster—especially as some political heavyweights of the day were openly opposed to his plans. In Nehemiah 6:1–14 we find some of the ploys Satan used to try to distract Nehemiah from his vision.

Distraction 1: Compromise
First of all, Nehemiah's enemies tried to compromise his vision. Sanballat, his chief opponent, extended the olive branch of peace: 'Come, let us meet together in one of the

villages on the plain of Ono,' he says (Neh. 6:2). Sanballat was offering to talk things through and perhaps to give his approval, but you can bet there would be strings attached.

He's really saying something like this: 'Nehemiah, I'm willing to concede that there may be some merit in this plan of yours. Perhaps I've been too hasty in opposing it. On the other hand, you're a pretty stubborn dude yourself. If you can just cool it a little on some of your more radical ideas, perhaps we can reach a compromise.'

Sanballat is offering respectability, which is the death of vision! Whenever we settle for the comfort of living without criticism, we settle for a life of non-achievement. Someone said: 'It's better to be criticised than ignored.' Someone else has written that, 'A great person is someone who knows how to build a sure foundation from the bricks others throw at him or her.' I believe it. Besides, no one ever built a statue to a critic—it's only the doers or the triers who are commemorated and celebrated. Don't allow those who feel threatened by your vision to draw you away from the task by offering a compromise.

What does Nehemiah the wall-builder say in response? 'Meet in Ono? Oh no!! I'm too involved in an important project to come to you' (Neh. 6:3). He recognised the importance of the work and of his part in it. He rejected anything less than the best. He'd face criticism if he had to—it would be worth it in the end.

Distraction 2: Accusation

Sanballat is a conniving creature. 'There's a rumour going around that you want to be king of Israel,' he sneers at Nehemiah. 'We know you're planning to revolt against the king of Assyria. He's not going to like that! Now come on, let's talk this out, shall we?' (Neh. 6:6–8)

Satan will try to wear us down with accusation if he can. 'If you keep up this project,' he'll say, 'you'll ruin your health.' 'If you stick with this vision you'll lose your family.' 'If you don't stop now, your finances will be destroyed.' And on it goes.

What is Nehemiah's response? 'Nothing like what you're saying is going to happen, you're making it up in your head' (Neh. 6:8). What authority! He doesn't waste time arguing the point, he just puts the accusation to rest. This is what the Bible tells us to do with unjust criticism. We are to tear down the strongholds of Satan, not negotiate with him (2 Cor. 10:4).

Vision will cost you some enemies. You just won't have time to waste on feelings of bitterness or revenge. Vindictiveness, if you allow it, will always occupy the space in your heart which should go to vision. Nehemiah turned to prayer for strength: 'O God, strengthen my hands' (Neh. 6:9 KJV).

Distraction 3: Infiltration

The last track of Sanballat's ploys is a subtle one. Having tried to sidetrack Nehemiah through an offer of compromise and respectability, having attempted to weaken his resolve through accusation, Sanballat now turns his attention to Nehemiah's closest friends. A man who is himself involved in the rebuilding comes to Nehemiah with news of a threat against his life. 'Nehemiah,' says this colleague, ' . . . Let's go inside the Temple and close the doors' (Neh. 6:10). Again, the bottom line is the same: drop your tools Nehemiah, leave the work, abandon the vision.

But Nehemiah is made of sterner stuff. 'Should a man like me [with my calling and responsibilities] run

37

away? Should I run for my life into the Temple? I will not go' (Neh 6:11). Nehemiah saw that this man had been hired to intimidate him and discredit him in the eyes of those he was leading (Neh. 6:13). What kind of leader would down tools and run when every other man on site was constantly in danger of attack?

Distractions will sometimes come through those close to you. In this respect vision will cost you some friends. Sometimes even the people closest to you will not appreciate the vision God has given you. They just can't feel as you do about it and may even try to hijack it. Joseph's brothers were so encouraged by his vision that they threw him into a huge rabbit hole (Gen. 37:23–24)!

How do people close to you become distractions? Sometimes a friend will have one foot nailed to the floor. You know the type: you give them counsel about a problem week after week after week but they never do anything about it. They just go around in circles wasting your time. Shake the dust off your Reeboks and get on with the vision! (Matt. 10:14)

Then, if you're a leader, there may be those who want to be your 'special friend'. They want to get closer to you than anyone else in the group. They want to monopolise your time and influence you to their way of thinking. They challenge your objectivity—you can't be impartial when you're living in someone's back pocket.

Or you may find that someone who wants to work closely with you is doing so out of ulterior motives. Perhaps this is his or her way of getting kudos in the church, and they'll drop you when something more important comes along. Or this may be their path to forming a romantic attachment with you! Beware.

Now I'm not suggesting we should give everyone

around us the Chinese water torture to make sure they're OK to work with. What I am saying is that we ought not to be ignorant of Satan's devices (2 Cor. 2:11). When you have a God-given vision, and you're forming strategies to turn the dream into reality, you are a target for the enemy. Just keep your wits about you and get on with the job.

2

Declare War—Declare Prayer

*They didn't actually see Him pray too often—He
likes to get away for that. Up on a mountain, under
a tree or in the solitude of the wilderness, that's
where He'd pray. None of this public, pious breast-
beating of the Pharisees. No, they didn't get invited
to all of His private meetings with the Father. But
they could see the results when He got back! The
lame could walk, the blind could see, the deaf could
hear—without a surgical implant. He could take a
hike on a lake, tell wind and waves to cool it and
bring people along to their own funerals. Whatever
happened on that mountain it produced amazing
power for good.*

Christianity is, by its very nature, heroic. Jesus offered
more than a programme of morals or a series of theological
concepts. He gave commands. He issued challenges
which only the very brave will undertake. Christianity is
not for wimps.

One of the most heroic aspects of Christian life is the
discipline of intercessory prayer. Throughout the ages,
both during and since Bible times, prayer has featured
prominently in every great move of the Spirit of God. As
one preacher put it, 'There have been great revivals with-

41

out much preaching, but there's never been a great revival without much praying!' John Wesley said, 'God does nothing except in response to prayer.' It's often been young leaders who have lit the fires of prayer across nations.

Intercessory prayer is one of the first activities Satan will try to attack in the church during times of revival. Sadly today there are many Christian leaders and potential leaders who want to enjoy victory without a fight, and blessing without a cost. It has often been this way throughout history. Just when God has needed intercessors the most, He's been unable to find any.

In the time of Isaiah the Lord was 'astonished that there was no one to intercede' for His people (Isa. 59:16 NASB). Ezekiel records that God 'searched for a man . . . who should build up the wall and stand in the gap', to plead for the salvation of Israel. Sadly, says the Lord, 'I found no one' (Ezek. 22:30 NASB).

Every great hero of faith in the Bible and church history has been an intercessor. John Wesley's heart bled for the state of backslidden England; William Booth cried out for the poor and oppressed of Britain; John Knox cried 'Give me Scotland or I die' and George Muller poured out his heart in prayer daily for the orphans of Europe.

In Scripture, Abraham interceded for Sodom and Gomorrah (Gen. 18); Daniel stood in the gap for rebellious Israel (Dan. 9) and Paul said he would go to hell himself if it would mean the salvation of his Jewish compatriots (Rom. 9:3). Jesus was, of course, the ultimate exponent of the intercessory ministry. Even today He lives to make intercession for us before God (Heb. 7:25).

You're Weird . . .

We sing about it, we speak about it, we even pray for it—but what is it? Revival, I mean. What does a revival look like? I think it's about the church catching on fire and burning out of control through the rest of society! We can't say we're in national revival until the culture outside the church is affected by what is happening inside the church.

I've been to South Wales a couple of times now and I've visited the Welsh rugby clubs. During some years, there were no finals played in certain leagues despite the fact that the Welsh treat their football as a surrogate religion. What closed down the competition? The Welsh revival. Taverns also closed as the Holy Spirit swept hundreds into the Kingdom in just a matter of months.

I want to live in that kind of environment, don't you? So, what does it take for us to see revival? This may surprise you, but I found my answer to that question in my school maths class. They told me there that two circles which have the same centre point are *concentric;* two circles with different centres are *eccentric*.

Think about it: 'eccentric' is a great word to describe what a Christian ought to be. There ought to be something just a little bit weird about me! I should be off-centre by world standards. As a follower of Jesus, my life is not centred around humanism or rationalism or hedonism or any of the other philosophical systems common in our world today. The centre of my world and thought is Jesus the Person. This will set me up in opposition to the world system (Rom. 8:7).

The apostle Peter tells me I am part of God's 'peculiar' people (1 Pet. 2:9 KJV). The next time someone points to you and says, 'You're weird!' point them to that verse and tell them: 'I have permission to be strange! What's your excuse?!'

Jonathon Edwards, a preacher who actually lived through a mighty revival, taught that God moved in response to 'extraordinary' prayer. I'd call it eccentric prayer—beyond the norm, over-the-top praying. I am convinced that many Christians and even church leaders settle for a prayer life which is far below God's best.

2 Chronicles 7:14 tells us that if we want to see revival and spiritual healing in our society, we must first humble ourselves, pray and seek God's face. Many people in our churches have never been encouraged to go beyond 'normal' prayer—a few careless lines recited at the mid-week prayer session before they rush off to supper at McDonald's—and get into 'eccentric' prayer, the seeking of God's face. What then does eccentric, intercessory, revival prayer look like?

The Pain, the Passion . . .

There are some important things you should know if you're going to change history through the power of intercession:

Revival prayer is challenging the status quo

I mentioned in the introduction the first time I saw a *Rocky* film. Everyone in the cinema was spellbound by the performance of Stallone playing one of the gutsiest street fighters ever. All except me. I couldn't see Stallone—as far as I was concerned, it was me up there, Mal Balboa, hero extraordinaire.

Many of the top rating films of our day feature heroes who challenge and change the status quo around them, whether it's a Balboa, a Rambo or a Robin Hood. Within every one of us lives a hero, a rebel. God has given us a hero-drive, which makes us different from the animal kingdom. Because many of us don't feel we're achieving much that's notable, we latch onto fantasy heroes who ride high in the world of films and music.

The intercessory prayer warrior is God's idea of a hero—like Jesus. Prayer is one way in which Christians can challenge and change the status quo. Prayer has changed the course of history—the histories of individual people and of nations—many times and continues to do so today. For too long the church has tried to squash the rebel in young people. Instead we should be teaching people how to rebel as Jesus did, to strike out against the things He too rejected—injustice, selfishness, hypocrisy and so on. We need to tap the rebel in our young people, turning their restlessness into creative prayer energy.

Revival prayer is declaring war on the works of Satan

Have you flicked through a comic book recently? Chances are you'll see a lot of pictures of warfare: warfare in past, present and futuristic settings. The warrior spirit is alive and thriving in today's culture. The films people watch and the video games they play are filled with armed conflict.

The church has often missed an important bridging point into youth culture in particular. While we've been concentrating on gentle Jesus meek and mild, young people have been living with Conan the Barbarian. The Bible clearly states that Christian life is in part warfare—a battle of good versus evil within the individual heart and a call to arms against the enemy of human souls.

Satan plays for keeps. Unfortunately some Christians seem to find his existence hard to believe in, or they think, 'If I ignore him, he'll go away.' C. S. Lewis found it easier to believe in Satan than in God for: 'Alas,' he said, 'I've had more to do with him.' There are too many Christians today who have forgotten how to make war, how to drive the enemy out of their territory and away from their God-given inheritance.

We need to get back to the kind of praying which rescues fast-lane, die-young kids and turns lives around. The kind of prayer the apostle James described as fervent prayer (Jas. 5:16 KJV). Whenever we pray with intensity, we are enforcing the victory which Christ has already won on the cross. When we declare God's word and His will in prayer we have all the authority of heaven to back us up. We are demolishing spiritual strongholds of the enemy and binding his effectiveness against the spread of the gospel.

Intercessory prayer is not for the faint of heart—it's for warriors.

Revival prayer is standing in the gap
If someone wrote a book about your life, what would they call it? How would you feel if your biography was entitled simply *Intercessor*? That's the name given to a book about the life of Rees Howells, the Welsh prayer warrior whose prayers not only birthed a powerful Bible College, which

trained the likes of Reinhard Bonnke, but also influenced the outcome of World War II.[1]

Howells described the first stage of intercession as identification—the willingness to put yourself in the other guy's Reeboks and pray from where he is standing. Howells taught that 'Intercession so identifies the intercessor with the sufferer that it gives him a prevailing place with God.'[2]

Isaiah was born a prince, an aristocrat, yet God told him to go barefoot and naked for three years as a warning to Egypt and Cush (Isa. 20:3–4). Hosea was told to marry a prostitute as a sign to Israel that God was willing to forgive her spiritual adulteries and take her as his bride (Hos. 1:2–3). Jesus 'made himself nothing' in order to identify with our problems, pains and temptations (Phil. 2:7).

In Joel 2:16–17 the prophet calls the priests of God to prayer on behalf of the lost house of Israel. They're told to 'weep between the temple porch and the altar' (NIV). The porch signifies a place afar off from God, where there is no salvation and no relationship with Him. The altar is the place of nearness to God, where forgiveness and cleansing are to be found.

In verse 16 the bride is commanded to come out of her bridal chamber and the groom out of his room. Literally speaking, God is saying that the honeymoon is over, it's time to get to work! Having already experienced the benefits that come through the altar, where Christ died, we are now commanded to stand in the gap for those who are still removed from His presence.

1. Norman Grubb, *Rees Howells, Intercessor* (Lutterworth Press, 1976).

2. Ibid. p. 89.

Intercession is about standing in the gap for friends and those we care about. God is counting on us. When you pray for a friend, understand that yours might be the only voice lifting that soul up to God.

Paul the apostle makes a remarkable statement in 1 Corinthians 3:9. He says that he and his fellow apostles are God's co-workers for the sake of the believers. It is an awe-inspiring concept—that Christians can work alongside the Lord in bringing His Kingdom into reality. Jesus Himself taught that the work of the Kingdom is one which He has entrusted into human hands. In Matthew 9:37–38, we are told that our prayers will lead to workers being sent into the harvest. In John 14:16, Jesus calls the Holy Spirit our 'paraclete', a Greek term meaning 'one who comes alongside to help'. For what purpose is the Spirit sent? To assist us, to work in co-operation with us in the work of God.

Unless we're willing to pray and then act upon those prayers, a generation might be lost to God. We might be the only real hope for the salvation of our friends and loved ones. Intercessory prayer is something which even the least talented, most introverted Christian can do well.

Revival prayer is intense

This kind of identification will call upon all of our reserves of compassion and strength. For Rees Howells, the second stage of intercession is 'agony'.[3] Real intercessory prayer often consumes everything we are. All of our faculties are involved—mind, body, emotions and spirit. The apostle Paul described intercessory prayer as a key part of his constant 'labour', his 'struggling' for the people he led (Col. 1:9, 29 NIV).

3. Grubb, op. cit. p. 86.

Hannah didn't want much out of life. She didn't need to win the lottery, she didn't care if she never featured on a Cosmo cover or made it into the Rock Music Hall of Fame. All she really wanted was to have a baby. But, sadly, she was barren. Living in pre-IVF times, she had only one place to turn for help: to God.

So she parked herself outside the temple and began to pour out her heart before the Lord in prayer. Hannah prayed as if her life depended on it. Eli, the friendly neighbourhood priest, saw her rocking back and forth in the dust and thought he'd encourage her. 'Woman, you're drunk!' he said (see 1 Sam. 1:13).

But was Hannah discouraged? No sir. She just went on praying until, in His own good time, the Lord came through with a son. Not just any ol' son either—this kid grew up to become Israel's prophet. God honoured the intensity of Hannah's prayers. We need people today who don't care what others think about the way they pray; gritty fighters who'll abandon their pride to see the answer through.

A teenager once asked Bob Pearce, the founder of World Vision, how he could become a man of God. Pearce replied: 'Find out what is breaking the heart of God and pray that it will break your heart also.'[4]

Revival prayer is determined

I've never given birth to a baby. Having babies is simply not one of my talents. But my wife has given me three very wonderful kids and watching her go through childbirth has taught me to respect the passion and the pain of childbirth. It's also taught me a couple of practical things

4. Bill Hogg, *Bill Hogg's Most Excellent Guide to Prayer* (Kingsway, 1992), p. 105.

about how babies come into the world. For example, I know that a mother-to-be can't simply walk into hospital and demand that her baby be born 'right now . . . or else!' Baby doesn't wear a Rolex.

A woman knows that childbirth involves giving up all rights to set time limits. The baby will arrive when it is ready and not before.

Intercessory prayer is not unlike childbirth in that respect. Once you set yourself to pray eccentrically for something, you must be content to hang in there until the answer comes in its appointed time. Let's be honest—sometimes the Lord seems to us to be a little on the slow side in His work. Consider how long it took for Jesus to arrive on the world stage. God in His wisdom waited thousands of years before revealing His Son. All that time the Divine Playwright was preparing the stage, setting the scene so that things were just right for the triumphant entry of the Star in His salvation drama.

Yet, 'when the right time came'(Gal. 4:4), God moved very quickly. Jesus was born, taught, worked miracles, died and rose again all within the space of just about 33 years. The world has never been the same since.

George Muller, the great orphanage-pioneer, prayed for one unconverted friend for something like sixty years. Even on his deathbed Muller still refused to stop believing for his friend's salvation. A short while after his death his friend came to Christ. Don't underestimate the power of persistence.

Jesus taught us that it's OK to be persistent in prayer (Luke 11:5–10) and God told the Jews to give Him 'no rest' until He'd fulfilled His promises in their land (Isa. 62:6–7 KJV). When we know a thing is in line with God's word and will for us, we should pray for it with patience and persistence. We should indulge in a little of what one writer calls 'holy violence'.[5] Too many revivals have been aborted or still-born simply because Christians gave up praying too soon.

Revival prayer is powerful

This over-the-top kind of prayer is effective. Rees Howells' Bible college prayed night and day throughout the closing stages of World War II. They intensified their efforts when it looked as if Britain herself might just be invaded during the now famous Battle of Britain.

The German Luftwaffe seemed to have the whole thing nicely wrapped up. They were within fifteen minutes of a glorious victory in the skies over London. Churchill's generals searched in vain for extra planes to meet the onslaught. The whole situation looked hopeless.

Then something strange happened—the Germans turned around and flew towards home. It was amazing, unbelievable! The only explanation Churchill's officers could offer was, 'divine intervention'. How right they were. Intercessors across the country, like Howells and his students, had been praying Britain through her darkest hour. After identification and agony comes authority! Revival prayer makes 'great things happen'(Jas. 5:16).

Youth leader and pastor, your prayer warriors need to be kept up to date whenever prayers are answered. If feedback is the 'breakfast of champions', it is the breakfast, lunch and dinner of prayer warriors. Don't expect people to continue praying fervently if you keep them in the dark about what their prayers are achieving in the real world.

---

5. Bill Hogg, op. cit. p. 93.

Whenever even the smallest answer arrives, share it with them. If you water prayer pygmies with a little encouragement, they soon become prayer giants.

Want to know more about the power of revival prayer? Read on, mighty warrior . . .

Some People Don't Know the Meaning of 'Can't' . . .

'It can't be done!' Ever had that line thrown at you? Encouraging, isn't it? Not really, but it can inspire you to prove the cynics wrong. Throughout the history of the church there have been brave men and women—many of them quite young—who have risen above the taunts and doubts of the cynics to bring mighty revival into being through prayer.

One of the greatest ways I know of motivating yourself to pray is through studying the lives of radical intercessors of old. There's no shortage of useful material, and you'll need to do some research for yourself (consult the reading list at the end of this book), but here are a few examples to point you in the right direction:

Bible characters
Men like Samuel, David, Jeremiah and Daniel, to name but a few, were all great men of prayer in their youth. Bible history bears record to the effectiveness of their intercession. Scripture should always be our starting point for any programme of study on any subject—and not least the subject of prayer.

The Moravians
Way back in 1722, before even Elvis Presley was born, a twenty-two-year-old East German named Ludwig von Zinzendorf established an Acts of the Apostles type of community. They were committed to living out the Kingdom of God in practical ways. A dedicated group of Jesus people, they initiated a prayer meeting which lasted for one hundred years. (And we find it hard to stay at it for one hundred minutes!) For a century, generations of rostered prayer warriors carried on an intense prayer battle on behalf of the nations of the world, and many missionaries were sent forth from their number. Some prayer meeting!

William Carey
The ministry of perhaps the greatest missionary to India began in England as young Bill Carey prayed intensely month after month for the people of far-away India—a place he'd never visited. Inspired by written accounts of Captain Cook's expeditions, Carey took a large map of the world and prayed fervently for each of the peoples in each of its various regions. That's how his passion for India was born—in prayer. He later taught himself Indian dialects and translated the Bible into these complex languages.

John Wesley
How would you like to turn a third of your nation to God? According to some historians that's basically what Wesley did. The founder of the Methodist movement is also accredited with having helped to save England from the kind of bloody social revolution that was turning France upside down. Not a bad résumé to carry into heaven!

Wesley preached over 50,000 sermons in his lifetime, many from the back of a horse. (He would probably have been a biker evangelist if he had lived today.) He wrote 233 books. His legacy to the world included 11,000 trained preachers and 135,000 followers at the time of his death. Each of his leaders was required to fast for two days and pray for hours each week, just as he did himself. He was, in all respects, a remarkable man. His constant prayer was: 'Lord, let me not live to be useless.'

George Whitefield
Prayer was a key ingredient in this man's life and ministry. He started preaching at twenty-one years of age and by the time he turned twenty-five he was preaching to crowds of 30,000. Amazing.

Charles Finney
This hero of latter-day revival didn't become a Christian until he was twenty-nine years of age, yet he went on to lead something like a half a million people to Christ. Eight per cent of his converts reportedly went on for God—that's not a bad retention rate. He was quite a sharp thinker and an authoritative preacher, yet before he commenced a crusade in any town or city, he would rent a room for a few days leading up to the meetings and would pray there for souls to be saved.

On more than one occasion, Finney's loud and energetic praying brought expressions of concern from worried passers-by who thought he might be in pain. He was—but not in the way they thought.

Praying Nash
You probably haven't heard much of old Nash. He was a

friend of Finney's. He wasn't a preacher, but Finney wouldn't have been half as successful without him. Nash would often accompany Finney as he travelled and would stay in his room to pray while the preacher reaped the harvest. Imagine having a nickname like 'Praying Steve' or 'Praying Jane'!

The Haystackers

Attention all students: start praying now! As a young college student in Massachusetts, USA, Samuel Mills would gather students together two afternoons per week for fervent prayer. One afternoon as he and four others were praying in open fields, a thunderstorm overtook them and they fled for shelter under a haystack. As the storm raged around them they experienced a new stirring of the Holy Spirit and began to cry out to God that He would send labourers from American colleges into foreign mission fields.

Two years later, Mills and his friends had established a prayer movement which spread across a great number of college campuses, a movement from which many well-known missionaries were eventually sent.

D. L. Moody

At the age of just twenty-one years, Moody pioneered a Sunday school ministry with just a few kids. By the time he was thirty-six it had grown to over 2,000 in attendance. In one twenty-week crusade in London alone, he ministered to 2.5 million (yes, million!) people. In his lifetime he led over a half a million people to Christ and prayer was central to his daily routine.

Evan Roberts

While still in his early twenties Evan Roberts, a Welshman,

was spearheading a revival which eventually touched many parts of the world. This great move of the Spirit began with a young man who, in his teens, would regularly walk the valleys of southern Wales weeping and crying out to God for the apostate nation in which he lived. The revival he helped to bring about through prayer caused the closure of normally packed taverns and rugby clubs.

David Brainerd

Here's a young man who was thrown out of Bible college, yet went on to become America's most beloved modern missionary. Early in his ministry the Holy Spirit laid hold of him and turned him into a nuclear reactor of faith. As he prayed he developed a passion for the Aucas of Ecuador and went to live among them. He died of TB when he was just twenty-nine, but his faith legacy lived on.

Smith Wigglesworth

How'd you like to be remembered as 'The Apostle of Faith'? Smith Wigglesworth from Britain was. He started his working life not as a preacher but as an uneducated plumber. In his early years of marriage he possessed no evident ability to speak in public and his wife was the preacher in the family. As the result of a powerful encounter with the Holy Spirit, however, Wigglesworth became one of the greatest healing ministries the world has seen in recent times. He claimed to have read no other book than the Bible and preached and practised a disciplined and vigorous prayer life.

Whenever young leaders have prayed with intensity and determination God has moved in power. A trip to the Christian bookshop or library will reveal many more historical examples with which you can inspire yourself and others to pray. Go for it!

How to Rewrite History . . .

Once you've taken some time to read up on the prayer warriors of old, you shouldn't have too much trouble feeling motivated to pray. Now it's important to find others who feel the same way as you do about intercession and get down to business together.

Remember the Marlboro Man from the old TV and cinema tobacco commercials? What a dude—strong, lean, confident and independent. He didn't say a thing, but the image said it all: he didn't need anyone else, he was completely self-sufficient. No emotional crutches (if you don't include the rolled-up weed hanging from his lip) and no strings attached. He didn't answer to anyone. A real man.

Is that really what maturity is about? I don't think so. Maturity is about recognising my reliance upon others, without failing to take responsibility for myself. There's not much you can achieve in life without the involvement of others. We draw from each other's strengths and cover for each other's weaknesses. Poor old Marlboro didn't know so much after all.

Like many other important things in life, intercessory prayer is most effective when it's done by a group. According to the Psalmist, God 'commands the blessing' upon those who work in unity with others (Ps. 133:3 KJV). The corporate prayer event is one of the ways in which we express that unity.

If you're a church leader or pastor please, please be

creative when you plan prayer events! So many leaders will take great care to plan just about every other kind of event but will leave the prayer programme looking wimpy and haphazard. Revival prayer is never boring and we must never make it seem that way.

A word to all the aspiring leaders out there: you can get a corporate prayer event happening yourself. Get some friends together and go for it—don't wait to be asked. Here are a few practical ideas for prayer events to start your creative juices flowing:

Prayer offensives

These may be planned and promoted as special prayer events at frequent intervals. Half-nights of prayer are probably the most popular kind of prayer offensive and one of these each month to six weeks can give the spiritual life of your youth group and its outreach capability a huge shot in the arm.

The format for a half-night of prayer might go something like this. Begin with full-on praise and worship, no holds barred. Follow twenty minutes of radical singing with a short inspirational message on prayer—no more than about ten minutes. Share about some hero of faith or a principle of effective prayer. Don't deliver a sermon, just pump some spiritual steroids into your warriors.

Once their engines are revving, map out the track ahead. List a few major things you'll want to pray for in the first prayer session. Be specific—people respond best when they know what it is you expect of them. Lead them in a quick starter prayer and then let them at it!

By the way, encourage your prayer group to intercede fervently with their body language as well as their words. Some people will enjoy sitting to pray, others will find kneeling the best way to motivate themselves to seek God. However, many others will pray more effectively while they walk around. Movement gets both the muscles and the brain going.

Also, remember that it's not irreverent to have everyone praying aloud all at once. God has absolutely no trouble hearing us all when we pray simultaneously. You won't hear God saying, 'Will you praying Koreans quieten down so I can hear the Aussies and the Brits?' So encourage people to go for it with all the energy they have in them.

After perhaps thirty minutes of intense prayer on the themes you've given—it might help to write them on a blackboard to keep them before the people—gather everyone together again. Sing a song or two and then share another brief message, this time perhaps only five minutes in length. Share some new prayer themes and then let them go again. This prayer session might last only twenty minutes, since concentration spans grow shorter as time goes by.

If you're praying for three or four hours, you'll need to allow times for quiet reflection too. Times when people can sit down and quietly meditate on what they've been praying for and, more importantly, whom they've been praying to! This is why members of the group should be encouraged to bring their Bibles to every prayer event. They will need time to seek God for themselves, space to recharge the emotional and spiritual batteries before launching into the battle once more.

Prayer offensives can become a major highlight of a youth or church programme. In fact, every youth pastor should make this his goal—to see a majority of his youth as excited about prayer events as they are about social events. If leaders treat prayer as a priority, and plan events well, they will reproduce after their own kind and 'grow' a harvest of warriors who can't wait for the next prayer night.

Prayer retreats (or, better still, advances)
Why not organise for your youth group to go away for a day or so to pray? Rent a large house, some caravans or a campsite by the beach, in the mountains or in the country, and devote a day and night to prayer. A certain amount of structure is needed on this kind of prayer camp, but don't overdo it. Allow some informality. Being able to relax, share and have fun is important on a prayer camp.

Pastor, every so often it pays to take your leaders away separately for their own prayer retreat. It need only be for a Friday evening into Saturday afternoon, but it's an exciting way to encourage prayer and to build relationships.

Praise concerts
I have found these to be among the most exciting and effective youth prayer events possible. Basically, praise concerts are just what the name suggests: concerts devoted to praise. The programme must be sharp and fast-paced. (When was the last time you saw the Rolling Stones stop a concert for announcements?!)

Five-minute testimonies, short Bible readings, music ministry from soloists or groups, can all be interspersed into the programme of praise, so that nobody really gets a chance to lose interest. The programme must always be arranged in such a way that it builds towards a great climax of intercession and a conclusion of celebration.

The first half of the night—say one hour or so—

should be more structured than the second part, which should allow more space for spontaneity. Even then, however, you must maintain a lead in proceedings. Don't let things get bogged down. Praise concerts, well run, can bring new spiritual breakthrough to a youth group and church.

Prayer warrior teams
Form crack squads of young people who see themselves as spiritual commandoes going behind enemy lines and plundering his kingdom. These people commit themselves to pray for a certain period of time each day on prayer themes which are given by the leadership at regular intervals.

The teams might have squad names which they choose themselves and, if you're the youth group leader, you might appoint a leader of each team to co-ordinate and strategise under your oversight. Warrior teams encourage a mutual support network which is vital to the growth of any youth group or church.

Whenever an answer to prayer comes through, be sure to give your warriors feedback. Meet with them regularly to encourage and stimulate them to believe God. Build a sense of camaraderie among them and make the prayer team something of which everyone will want to be a part.

Prayer chains
Call them what you like, these are a fantastic means of getting people involved in ongoing prayer. Whenever a need arises in the youth group, the church or the community, the first person on the list contacts the next, and so on until all are aware of and are praying for that need. Make sure these prayer chain members don't treat their link as a

medium for gossip. There is no such thing as 'Godly gossip'. Remember to give feedback on answers to prayer.

'Shake the Planet' events

Buy a large map of the world and commission teams of people to find out as much as they can about each of its major regions and its needs. Have them present their major findings at a special Planet-Shaker event where the emphasis will be on building a world vision in Christian hearts. You may need to give a typed outline of the kinds of information you're looking for from each group, stating clearly the aims of the whole exercise, which is to help the youth group to know how to pray for each part of the globe.

Do some research and familiarise yourself with the unreached people groups of the world—those ethnic groups which have no real gospel witness in their tongue or cultural setting. Have groups of people adopt one of these people groups as a prayer target in their individual and corporate prayer lives. Use the information gathered in your special prayer emphasis events, praying for a major region over a period of weeks or even months. Who knows how many missionaries and mission-support workers may go forth from your group in future, simply because you encouraged a world prayer vision in the church?

Prayer marches

Why not organise a march through your city or town, singing radical songs and stopping to pray at certain points along the way? Stop outside the places of local government as well as any X-rated cinemas or bookshops dealing with pornography. In this way an outreach march doubles as a prayer event—and it's gutsy, risky living.

There are so many ideas you can implement to build the prayer profile of your youth group and church. There are only two rules in planning a prayer event: it must be creative and it must be a part of an overall programme. Loosely thrown together and infrequent prayer events are of no use when it comes to building a lasting heart for prayer. Consistency is a key.

Nothing is taught until something is learned, so just keep doing the same thing in as many different ways as possible, and eventually the idea of prayer will catch on. When it does, you have a spiritual power station on your hands!

You Can't Lead the Team from the Bench . . .

When it comes to prayer, there's only one way to lead— from the front. I know how easy it is to teach others to do one thing and then personally do another. That was the way of the Pharisees. Like the fig tree Jesus cursed, they professed more than they possessed.

Be a prayer warrior yourself, both in public and in your private walk with God. People are looking for heroes upon which to model their lives.

It was George Bernard Shaw who remarked: 'The reasonable man adapts himself to the world; the unreasonable man persists in trying to adapt the world to himself. Therefore all progress depends on the unreasonable man.'

Be unreasonable, eccentric and peculiar when it comes to prayer. Be a prayer hero to younger Christians— give them a high standard to aim for. They will respond and the world around will hear about it.

Declare war—declare prayer! Think on these words which were written about Rees Howells the Welsh bombshell:

> [The Holy Spirit] has no hearts upon which he can lay his burdens, and no bodies through which he can suffer and work, except the hearts and bodies of those who are his dwelling place . . . [The intercessor] moves God. He even causes him to change his mind.[6]

6. Grubb, op. cit. pp. 87, 89.

3

Speaking in Nobody's Sleep

He was not a rock star. He didn't record a chart-stopping hit or write a best-selling book. He had no fan club and they didn't ask him to appear on network TV. He wasn't nominated for an Oscar and did not run for political office. They didn't sell his merchandise at public appearances and he didn't lend his name to any popular cause. Yet this one man changed the course of history.

Thousands of people flocked to Jesus everywhere He went. Crowds would follow Him for days, sometimes even forgetting to go home for food (Mark 8:2). Sometimes the only way you could get near Him when He was teaching was to abseil through the roof! (Mark 2:4). Or you'd have to climb a tree just to catch a glimpse of Him through the adoring crowd (Luke 19:4).

The poor and broken, the rich and powerful, the learned and the ignorant—they all turned up at his 'gigs'. But why? What was it that held them? His miracles? Certainly that was part of the attraction, but sometimes He would not heal for hours on end. So why did they stay?

Simple—they loved His preaching and teaching. Crowds listened to Jesus 'with pleasure' (Mark 12:37) because 'He taught as one who had authority and not as their teachers of the law' (Matt. 7:29 NIV). While their lawyers and religious leaders managed to bore them to tears with eloquent but shallow rhetoric, Jesus moved them with His untrained but passionate speeches. He could make you cry and then make you want to cheer. His stories were charged with emotion and packed with real-life experience. His proverbs were pithy and He could be as sharp as a rapier or as soft as a feather. Somehow He made it seem as if you couldn't miss what He'd say next.

In comparison, many of today's preachers have largely lost the attention of the masses, who view their pro-nouncements as uninspiring if not irrelevant. Sadly, I have to agree with an old wag who said that, unlike Jesus, 'Many modern preachers speak in other people's sleep.'

The greatest leader who ever lived knew the power of the spoken word—He was first and foremost a preacher. For him, preaching was more effective than music, or writing or any other style of communication. If there'd been a more powerful way to spread the Good News, God's own Son would not have come as a preacher.

Like Jesus, the apostle Paul relied heavily on preaching to bring people to God. In Acts 20 we find him saying his final, emotion-charged farewells to the leaders of his churches in Ephesus. 'You know that I have not hes-itated to preach anything that would be helpful to you,' he says, 'but have taught you publicly from house to house . . . I have not hesitated to proclaim to you the whole will of God' (Acts 20:20, 27 NIV). Paul was proud to be a preacher of the will of God. He knew the power of the message he preached (Rom. 1:16) even though some considered it to be 'foolishness' (1 Cor. 1:18).

Even in this age of the high-tech, the hands-free and the environmentally friendly, preaching is still the most effective way of sharing the heart of God with others. Preaching, when done under the inspiration of the Holy Spirit, changes human lives in a way that even music, that second language of our generation, cannot equal.

These days, people need hope more than anything else. Our pagan Western society offers what seems to be a myriad of choices for lifestyle and belief. Moral absolutes are unfashionable, situation ethics have taken root in the modern mind. We celebrate the social 'liberation' of the 60s, 70s and 80s. But if we were liberated then, we're confused now. Without moral fibre and framework the thatchwork of society has begun to unravel.

Preaching is the most forceful, forthright and no-nonsense way of communicating hope known to man! There simply is no more dynamic a way of opening hearts to the possibility of a better life—a better life on the other side of repentance.

What is Preaching?

Throughout history various preachers gave their thoughts on what preaching is all about. Phillip Brooks taught that preaching is truth poured through personality, that the audience hears as much of the man as they do of the message.

Bishop William A. Quale obviously agreed with this definition. He said that preaching is not the art of making a sermon and delivering it, rather it is 'the art of making a preacher and delivering that!'

I've also heard it said by more than one teacher that preaching should be about a manifestation of the incarnate Word from the written Word via the spoken word.

Here's the bottom line: preaching is about communicating all that's in the heart of God to the people that He loves.

The New Testament uses three main Greek words to describe preaching. The first is *euaggelizo* (Luke 4:18), from which we get 'evangelism'. This speaks of preaching good news, preaching about Christ and what He came to do. That is a key to great preaching: keeping Christ central to the message.

The second word is *kerugma* which speaks of proclamation (Mark 16:15). It literally means the proclamation issued by a herald of old. You know, 'Hear ye! Hear ye!' and that kind of thing. This reminds us of the prophetic responsibility of the preacher—he or she must get the word out just as he received it—without compromise, because he or she is accountable to a higher authority.

The third New Testament word for preaching (Acts 9:27) is, wait for it, *parrhesiazomai* (try saying that one quickly with a mouth full of marbles!). It means 'to be bold in speech'. I read somewhere that the preacher's job is to 'comfort the afflicted and afflict the comfortable'. There is a courageous confrontation involved somewhere in all good preaching, because the evil on people's hearts will not want them to swallow truth when they hear it (see Jer. 1:8; Josh. 1:5–6).

What can preaching achieve? It can inspire, producing faith which reaches out to God. It can motivate, bringing changes in the way we live. It can reveal God, not in some abstract, intellectual fashion, but in a very personal way—bringing not just the spark of information but the fire of revelation. It can confront us, bringing us to see our own awful need of God and it can bring hope for our salvation. It can produce balance, tearing down false doctrines which would lead us astray. It can teach us practical principles for a lifestyle which is pleasing to God. In short, preaching can accomplish in us what no other form of communication can.

If you read the heavy-duty, industrial-strength books on preaching, you'll find that this art can take on many different forms. There are a few major forms a message can take. It might be a textual sermon—one which breaks down just one verse or two, digging out the central truth. A message might be expository, opening up a passage or whole chapter or book and identifying the major themes therein. Biographical messages study Bible characters, drawing truth from key events and experiences in their lives. Analogical messages compare passages to draw out the similarities and differences, say, between different characters. Sometimes the Holy Spirit will speak through an extemporaneous message—one for which there's been no formal preparation, but which is born right there and then.

Preaching can take many forms, but unless the speaker appreciates the power of his calling, it will all be worth nothing.

John Mott, the eminent churchman of the nineteenth century, made the following comment on the history of Christianity: 'Whenever the church has failed, it has failed because of inadequate leadership.' One of the keys to effective leadership is the accurate and passionate passing on of ideas. We need leaders in the church today who know the power of preaching—speakers who boldly and skilfully use language to reveal God's good news. C. H. Spurgeon, the great revivalist of old, told his Bible students: 'If you're called to be a preacher, don't stoop to be a king!'

If you're going to be a good leader, you have to learn the skills of good communication. There are a few simple things you can do to develop as a preacher:

Beware the Dump Truck . . .

It's 6 p.m. and you're returning home from an incredibly hard day at work. Through the blanket of city smog you can just make out the orange orb of the sun sinking slowly in the west. You're really looking forward to getting into some non-work gear and throwing down a hearty meal. It's great to be going home.

Suddenly, as you turn the corner into your street, you notice something very different about your front lawn. It's covered in dirt—well, soil to be precise. As you get closer you see that it looks like high quality soil, real A-grade stuff. But you spent all last weekend trimming the lawn— now it's buried under a foot of unexpected earth. There's a truck pulling out of your drive. The sign on its cab reads: *'Dirty Trix Deliveries: We don't wait to be asked.'*

The driver is smiling and waving at you. You just stare back at him, absolutely dumbfounded. Then you see the bill taped to your front door.

'No need to thank me,' says the truck driver, with a sickening grin.

'But . . . but . . . I didn't order this stuff!' you protest.

'I know,' he grins, 'but you sure needed it, didn't you, pal? No need to thank me. See you later . . . '

Of course you have no intention of thanking

anyone. Given half a chance you'd give him a little delivery of your own. It's not the soil that annoys you—it's the *method of delivery*. Someone has just assumed you wanted this stuff and dumped it on you without any respect for your feelings and thoughts.

That's the way it is for many people when we preach the gospel at them rather than to them. We can be very good at telling people what we want them to hear—what we're comfortable telling them—and not what they need to hear. So we leave people feeling as if we've dumped something in their laps and run.

'Preachers often try to answer questions which nobody is asking!' remarked some great wit, expressing in a different way the idea of 'preaching in other people's sleep'.

Sadly, not enough modern preachers are also good communicators. Some preachers keep talking when people have stopped listening. Who wants to talk while everyone around you is nodding off? The word 'communicate' comes from 'commune' which means 'to have an intimate discussion with a friend or one's heart; together'. Both come from the Old French word *comuner*, 'to share'. Communication is a two-way street.

Remember this, O ambitious preacher: *nothing is taught until something is learned.* Communication is basically about using words to mobilise people into action. It's not crowds which make a great speaker, it's what leaves with the crowds. John F. Kennedy said of Churchill that during England's darkest nights he mobilised the English language and sent it into battle.

The true measure of a good speaker is whether or not anyone actually does what he or she suggests! One friend of mine was pastoring a large youth group when some of his kids asked him, 'Why do you keep sharing the same basic message over and over again?' 'I'll keep preaching it,' he retorted, 'until you do something with it!'

Unless people allow you to affect their thinking and actions, all your preaching will be just so much hot air. However, people won't allow you to influence them unless they think you have their best interests at heart, unless you're speaking from a position of respect for them. Preachers need to be listeners first.

I don't know if it's possible to have favourite books of the Bible but, if it is, two of my favourites would be Romans and Hebrews. Christians through the ages have clung to these books during times of confusion, because they give us such magnificent pictures of the ministry of Jesus. Hebrews speaks of Jesus as our High Priest, the one who has made a once-for-all-time sacrifice of Himself as the Lamb of God and has torn in pieces the curtain which kept us out of God's holy presence. Romans, on the other hand, teaches of the Christ who delivers us from slavery. He has paid the price to ransom us and has now freed us to be love slaves of our Father in heaven—a far better master than the one we knew before.

Both books are written about the same person and they're both divinely inspired. Yet they look at Jesus from very different angles. Why is this?

Hebrews and Romans were written to people from different backgrounds. For the Hebrew Christians the temple worship of Old Testament days was not a dry and dead idea learned from dusty history books. They lived with temple worship. They'd grown up with it. Now, said the writer of Hebrews, they had a new high priest who stood before God, interceding for them. He had made a once-for-all-time sacrifice for their sins.

On the other hand, what your average Roman knew about high priests and Jewish temples could be written on the back of a postage stamp in block letters! So in his letter to the Christians at Rome, Paul describes Christ's ministry in terms of the slave trade—something which went on constantly around them.

Each author tailored his message to fit the hearers. These writers were thinking about the needs of their readers. They weren't simply writing clever essays for no one in particular. In the same way, we modern preachers should get to know the values, experiences and needs of the people we want to reach. Otherwise people will feel that we're just getting something off our chests, fulfilling some sense of duty, meeting the demands of conscience. Instead of reconciling people to God, we'll only alienate them further.

I'm not for a moment suggesting that there should be no confrontation in our preaching. In fact, that's where too many speakers fall short of their call—they fail to take the risk of really laying the truth on the line and provoking a response. But to speak the truth without love, without compassion and empathy, is not God's way at all (1 Cor. 13:1). Old fashioned courtesy will not go astray in modern preaching—we must earn the right to be heard.

Invest in a Hearing Aid . . .

The good church folk in London were doing handstands down the aisles when they first heard about the people being saved in Ethiopia. According to their missionaries in this poor African country, many long years of preaching had finally paid off with 30 people coming to Christ.

The good Christians of England sent over some trunks filled with fine 'Christian clothes'—tailored suits and pretty dresses for the natives to wear to church on Sunday mornings. Before long, there were 30 rather odd-looking Africans going to church in the best second-hand European gear. They would arrive for church every Sunday morning at 11 a.m., in the heat of the day, looking for all the world like English churchgoers with great suntans.

Then the second world war broke out. The missionaries had to leave as Mussolini's armies marched in. They imagined their little flock being persecuted, scattered and eventually wiped out. Years later, after the end of the war, they were able to return. They couldn't believe what they saw! Their tiny Christian outpost had turned into a thriving community of believers. Their number had grown from 30 to 15,000!

The only tool the natives possessed for evangelism was the word of God—scraps of gospel passages left in the rush of the missionaries' departure. This part of the country was enjoying spiritual revival. The spiritual climate had definitely changed. But so had a couple of other things.

For one, the Christians no longer dressed in suits and dresses to go to church. They simply dressed as they'd always done—sparingly! They'd found no mention of wearing European clothes in the Bible so they'd simply abandoned the idea. And they no longer went to church at 11 a.m. on Sunday. Instead, they met late on Sunday evening after the sun had retired for the day. The Bible didn't say church should start at a specific time, so they'd decided to meet when the people of their villages were most active and ready for a praise party. They had culturalised the practice of their faith and as a result had led thousands more to Christ.

According to the apostle James, Christians should be quick to hear and slow to speak (Jas. 1:19). Listening is the first step in good communication. Had these well-meaning missionaries been listening a little harder they might have heard how out of tune their culture sounded in the ears of these black Africans.

People in different cultural groups think and express their ideas in different ways. In order to present the gospel in a relevant way, we will need to decipher the cultural codes around us. All preachers need to be involved in ongoing research into the thoughts, attitudes and needs of the world around them. Research is a preacher's 'hearing aid'. One great preacher of old said: 'You can only reach the contemporary generation if you preach with a Bible in one hand and a newspaper in the other.' Here are some pointers to get you started:

Understand the purpose of research

The major benefit to be derived from research is a 'feel' for the world we are trying to reach. Many young preachers bore people to tears with meaningless statistics, which they fail to link with anything really practical. Research allows us to keep in touch with the attitudes and behaviour of *real* people—statistics are just abstractions for human lives.

As we grow in our understanding of the pressures people face, we are ready to allow the Holy Spirit to break our hearts, to birth real compassion in our hearts—and we should never preach to people we don't care about! (Plastic has a certain, easily detected smell.)

Research is something we should be doing

constantly—watching, reading and listening ourselves into awareness. Of course the best research will always be mixing with real people. Living, breathing human beings are the best sources of information about humanity and its needs and problems. Don't completely shut yourself away in some cloistered study and hope to receive revelation only from heavy times. Get out where the real people live and move and have their being!

One pastor of a country church related to me how he would sometimes visit the local school and just sit around talking to the kids during lunch break. He started by mixing with young people from his church but before long other kids were starting to relate to him. He learned a great deal about youth culture just by talking with those students. Today he has a thriving youth programme in that community. All the reading in the world cannot replace mixing with real people in real situations.

Specify the kind of material you need
Every so often you will want to make a study of a particular issue. That's when you need to discipline yourself to stick to the subject and not to be sidetracked by irrelevant material. In research, as in writing, what you leave out can be just as important as what you put in. Researching must always be our servant, never our master—it is a means to an end, so keep the end, the goal, in mind.

Identify the best places to look
Once you've decided what types of information you're after you need to hone in on the most productive sources of material. You won't learn about modern music simply through reading books by musicologists—you'll need to hear a few song lyrics. And you can't hope to know what's

happening in youth unemployment unless you've read up-to-date government data on the subject. Find the right source: government departments, special interest groups, charities, local libraries, video and music outlets and your friendly neighbourhood newspaper stand—they're all excellent places to look, depending on what you need.

Keep accurate files

Unless you're blessed with the memory of a medium-sized computer, you'll need some way of storing the material you collect. Personal computers have made this much easier today, but even this method of storage often needs backup with traditional filing systems. You can file on cards, in exercise books and in scrapbooks filled with useful newspaper and magazine clippings.

Write on everything you keep: any clippings should have the source, the title and the date listed on them. (It's always courteous to give credit for a direct quote or a piece of research if you've taken it from someone else, especially if you come to write about it.) File cut-out items in manila folders which have key themes or categories written on them: e.g. 'family issues', 'youth suicide', 'interesting Bible facts'. You can file videos and cassettes using the same principle.

Worthwhile books should be scribbled in—provided they belong to you, of course. You need to make simple notes down the sides of pages and cross-reference information on one page with similar themes in other parts of the book. This makes it easy to regain access to the key ideas. Whenever you read a *really* helpful book you should keep a written summary of it—note down just the important points from each chapter, along with some of your responses, and file it all under one of your broad categories. Also, take note of other titles listed in the book's bibliography section. Get the help of your library or bookshop in tracking them down.

All this work really is worth it, if you treat research as an ongoing priority over a period of time. You can even enlist the help of friends in collecting material. Remember though: *research is a servant.* It only fulfils its purpose when it makes you a better communicator.

Develop a good library

We live in the age of information. Knowledge and the ability to share it are the great trading commodities of this era in history. Every Christian communicator needs to be a voracious reader, because we won't take our world for Christ with air bubbles between our ears.

Your library should at least include books from each of the following categories: discipleship, doctrine, biography, general reference (encyclopedia, atlas, dictionary), Bible reference, Bible commentary, letters of famous people, psychology, sociology (culture), novels, philosophy, special interest (hobbies, etc.).

Become a regular subscriber to certain magazines and newspapers too.

You're Not God's Cartoonist!

Ever seen one of those awful, twisted cartoons of politicians they feature in newspapers? Ugly, aren't they? It's amazing how much of a laugh you can get when you exaggerate a few facial features in that way. It could get kind of annoying after a while, though, if you were the subject of the mockery.

That's how God may feel when we preach inaccurately, when we fail to use 'the true teaching in the right way' (2 Tim. 2:15; see also 2 Pet. 3:16). There's not a preacher alive who hasn't made a 'bloomer' now and again. We've all had days when we've misquoted Scripture or even unwittingly misrepresented the meaning of a verse by taking it out of context. Some have done it on purpose—like the old bootlegger who justified his booze-making by misquoting Psalm 23: 'He leadeth me beside the still!'

We've all made mistakes, but it's important that we learn from them and don't go putting words in God's mouth. When we force the Bible to say something we want it to say—what scholars call 'eisegesis'—we're drawing cartoons rather than portraits of the Lord. In fact, that's one of the major reasons God continually disciplined His people of Israel in the Old Testament. It wasn't just that He liked to see them squirm—He knew that other nations were watching them and following their lead. Whenever Israel went off into sin people around them would begin to think that God approved of their behaviour. Before long, all the world had would be a caricature, a twisted picture of God's nature.

Whenever we're interpreting a passage of Scripture we must ask ourselves two basic questions: *what is the writer saying?* and *what is the writer saying to me?* We start by seeing the passage through the eyes of the writer and the original readers or hearers. What did it mean to them? How did they interpret it? We might need to read up on the language, culture and local customs of the day so that we understand the mindset of the writer and his immediate audience. Bible dictionaries and atlases are good value here.

Imagine some of the cruel things people could do with our letters if they dug them up in a thousand years' time. They could twist our language, our slang, our expressions to suit whatever meaning they wanted—we'd be outraged. Just a little study on what life and language were like in the late twentieth century would easily set them straight.

Some of those futuristic snoops might even decide to play games by playing with the order of the words and sentences, or cutting sentences in half. Preachers sometimes do this with the Bible—they build a doctrine on just one verse, or they quote just the first half of a sentence if that will back up their point of view. We have to see any one verse as part of a chapter, the chapter as part of a book, the book as part of a unified whole—the Bible. That's the kind of respect God wants for His word.

It's only after we see a passage in this light that we can really apply it to today. If we keep this simple process in mind, we will accurately present the word of God and not just the opinions of preachers.

Allowing the Bible to speak to us in this way is called 'exegesis'. Drawing caricatures is OK for political cartoonists but not for God's mouthpieces!

4

Life's Too Short to be
Boring . . .

There's only one group of people you don't want healed
while you preach—the insomniacs! What's the point of
being mind-numbingly well read and incredibly well
informed if you then put your audience to sleep with your
presentation?

We preachers must never bore people in the name of
the most fascinating person who ever walked the planet—
Jesus Christ. Let me pass on some tips which have been
learned from hard experience. These will help you to keep
the wolves of boredom and restlessness at bay so that
people stay with you right to the conclusion of your
message.

Speak the whole council of God
Sometimes young preachers get a little carried away just
preaching on their favourite subject. What people need to
hear is the word of God on a wide variety of day-to-day
concerns.

Paul told the leaders of the church in Ephesus that
he'd never failed to tell them all they'd needed to hear,
even if that meant rebuke (Acts 20:20, 27). As preachers
we are 'watchmen' for the people God loves, warning them

81

where danger lies ahead (Ezek. 3:17). It costs us to be that honest with people. Most people know David Wilkerson for the work he did among New York's street gangs and drug addicts during the early sixties. His ministry there was immortalised in the film and book called *The Cross and the Switchblade*. He was almost a Christian 'star' for a time, with people inviting him to speak all over the USA and the world.

Then he wrote a book called *The Vision* in 1973. It was a book written from David's heart and contained some very forthright prophetic warnings about what might happen in America if her people did not turn back to God. Suddenly, the popular evangelist was not so popular. He had written a book which wasn't all that comfortable to read and people did not want to hear its solemn message.

Nicky Cruz describes David Wilkerson this way: 'David Wilkerson is an evangelist and a pastor—he's a shepherd who deeply loves his flock—not a Jeremiah or a John the Baptist thundering about impending doom.'[1] David himself says:

> In the pulpit I always want to encourage people. So, when I have a burden to speak out against something, I find myself saying, "God, nobody wants to hear that. Let me preach something nice." And if I shrug off the message, the Holy Spirit will convict me so strongly that I can't sleep . . . it just burns.

David Wilkerson does not see himself as a prophet, but as an evangelist.[2] He is now pastoring the Times

1. Nicky Cruz, *A Final Warning: David Wilkerson* (Kingsway Publications, 1992), p. 99.

2. Ibid. p. 103.

Square Church in New York, and has a shepherd's heart for the broken and lost of that city. But when he feels strongly that some aspect of the whole word of God is not being preached, he is willing to take the risk of preaching it. Many of the predictions he made in *The Vision* have come to pass.

We need that kind of boldness in our preaching. Don't get into areas of condemnation, but make sure you preach a full balance, leaving out nothing that people need to be told. It is truth (not half-truth) which makes us free (John 8:32).

Don't preach to people you don't care about

George Whitefield was not an angel as a kid. He was a self-confessed liar, thief and gambler. Yet he became one of the greatest preachers of the eighteenth century. Winkey Pratney has this to say about Whitefield's preaching:

> His sermons were filled with immense feelings and pathos. He commonly wept profusely in the pulpit; Cornelius Winter, who later often travelled with him, said he had not seen him get through a sermon without a tear. This was no affectation; he felt deeply for the souls before him. His sincerity awakened affections . . . It smoothed down prejudices; they could not hate a man who wept so much over their souls.[3]

The apostle Paul understood this kind of passion:

---

3. Winkey Pratney, *Revival* (Whitaker House, 1983), p. 92.

I have great sorrow and always feel much sad-
ness . . . I would even wish that I were cursed and
cut off from Christ if that would help them [the
unsaved Jews] (Rom. 9:2–3).

Always remember that for three years, day and
night, I never stopped warning each of you, and I
often cried over you (Acts 20:31).

Jesus told us to pray for our enemies and those who
abuse us (Matt. 5:44). He knew that it is only as we pray
for our enemies that we come to love them. Prayer is an
investment we make in someone's life—the greater the
investment we make, the more we care about that person
and want to protect our investment.

Throughout the ages, great church leaders have felt
moved with compassion for those to whom they ministered. Evan Roberts, John Knox, Charles Finney and many
others were men whose compassion was born out of
prayer. In Genesis 30:1, Rachel cried, 'Give me children,
or I'll die!' I'm sure that if more of us preachers had that
same passion for souls, we might see more 'children' born
to us!

Before you speak to any people about God, speak to
God about the people. Pray for them until you feel a bur-
den of compassion.

'The preaching which kills,' observed one teacher of
old, 'is prayerless preaching. Without prayer the preacher
creates death, and not life.' Even strangers in your
audience can mean a lot to you if you've interceded in
private prayer. Most people will give you a hearing if they
think you honestly care for them.

Be honest, but be hopeful

People turn you off pretty quickly if they think you're only being half honest with them.

Life is not as easy as some preachers like to make out. Not everyone who prays for physical healing receives it here and now, and not every person who has real faith will wear a diamond ring and drive a Ferrari!

Dr Billy Graham has been around a long time! Listen to his words: 'I've listened to too many sermons . . . and seen too many Christian films with happy-ever-after endings.'[4] Becoming a Christian, he says, isn't the end of your problems, it's the beginning of your facing up to them.

Dr Graham issues a challenge to the church and to preachers: 'Why must we pretend with each other? Why must we wear assumed smiles of victory in our public gatherings and weep tears of loneliness and anger when we are alone?'[5] Why do we pretend that life is all roses and no thorns? That following Christ makes us superior to other human beings and places where we'll never really have another problem? That Christians don't make mistakes the way other people do?

The world's greatest living evangelist continues: 'Once we confess the fact that we Christians, too, still sin [we might add: and suffer], we see unbelievers in a new light—and they see us in a new light. We do not look down on their sinfulness from any position of arrogance.'[6]

Of course, the great thing about being a Christian is

---

4. Billy Graham, *Approaching Hoofbeats: the Four Horsemen of the Apocalypse* (Avon Books, 1983), p. 93.

5. Ibid. p. 99.

6. Ibid. p. 100.

that if we suffer we will experience God's grace to carry us through to victory. There's always hope if you're God's child. We have the right to ask God for a way out, but even if a way doesn't become obvious, there can be a purpose in our pain, a purpose which carries us through! (Remember Jesus' prayer in the Garden of Gethsemane?)

In the midst of our honesty about life, we must always preach faith in a mountain-moving God. Faith first acknowledges that there is a problem, then entrusts the solution to God. Preaching faith is not difficult. It involves making the Bible's miracles 'come alive' in their context and then, by sharing modern miracle stories, showing that God is still doing the same things today. We should encourage people to ask for their answer, then we must teach them the right way to ask—not arrogantly, as if God were an 'automatic teller machine', but with humility and childlike trust. Most of all, we must explain that it's not our faith alone which brings an answer—God acts because He is compassionate.

Get their attention!

This is the TV generation. We are competing for the attention of a generation raised on fast-paced films, aggressive music, colourful advertising and video games which bend the mind. We just can't afford to have people switch us off before we've even started.

We can learn a lot from TV producers and writers. They're not content just to let an audience drift into their programme. They know that unless they can grab the attention of a viewer in the first scene, they'll never get a second chance. So they make sure that in the first few minutes something fairly dramatic happens to involve the audience. They create a sense of tension which holds you through the first commercial break into the next scene. You may even be able to guess at the outset how the story will end—many TV tales are fairly predictable—but you're left wondering how it's all going to fall into place, and the tension holds you.

That's the way you should launch a talk: with a punchy introduction which involves your audience and makes them curious about what comes next. If you want to die in public, try something like this: 'Tonight I'm going to talk about The West Wing Wall of Moses' Tabernacle and the typological significance of each nail with reference to prophetic scripture . . . ' Bingo, you've struck out already! You need to make people think that if they tune out now they're going to blow a major opportunity for growth and help.

There are basically two approaches to winning the attention of an audience in this TV generation. The one you use depends largely on the type of hearer you're dealing with. The first involves using the Bible as your starting point. Here you will be working a Bible text back into everyday life and experience. The secret of this approach is to make Bible characters come alive in their context and then make them alive in our environment. This may involve dramatising Bible stories (without over-doing it).

How would you feel if, right now, before you finished this chapter, the doors of your room were kicked in and in marched a squad of Chinese paratroopers? How would you feel if these guys pushed you out the door at bayonet point, threw you into a Chinese truck and drove you to the airport where a Chinese plane was waiting to fly you to Beijing—one way? There, in a dungeon under Tiananmen Square, the commander tells you, in very broken English, that your home has been burned to the ground, your property confiscated and your family locked away where you'll never see them again? Now, he says, you're one of the 'privileged few' who've been chosen for 'reprogramming' as Chinese citizens, to work the rest of your days in the steamy roadside restaurants of Beijing? How would you feel?

You'd probably feel much the same as three young men did in Daniel chapter one . . . and I've used this kind of scenario many times in my preaching about Daniel. You didn't think of it as an introduction to a talk, did you? You weren't expecting it. You were just hooked and carried along by it all, before you even knew what was happening. Your imagination was switched on. That's what good introductions are all about. You don't get two chances to make a first impression!

The second approach to introducing a message is to start from the opposite end—to begin with the everyday experience of the hearer and work back to the Bible. Working from stories or statements about human experience can be a great way of ensuring that you trap your audience right from the start, especially when you're talking to an unchurched or youth audience.

Jesus often used this approach when He taught. Some modern Bible scholars believe that the story of the Prodigal Son was most likely told when Jesus was in a farming region near the site of the ten Greek cities which were known collectively as the Decapolis. These ten cities were situated on a high plain which overlooked a valley where Jewish farmers lived and worked. The cities, like modern ones, were filled with all the latest in modern Greek thought and with plenty of promiscuous living. Many a young man would have left his father's farm to

seek the high life in the big cities. Can you imagine the
impact Jesus' story would have made on the farmers who
first heard it? It would have related so well to their situation. He didn't expect them to start where He was at. He
started His teaching with a story about their everyday
experience.

We've used TV drama and sitcoms as a model for
introducing a subject. There's another thing we can learn
from TV writers: they're not content to grab the attention
once, at the beginning of a programme, and then let it slip
away. They grab attention, then grab it again, then grab it
again. Just when interest might be flagging, or proceedings are about to break for a commercial, something
dramatic or funny will happen to keep you interested
enough to come back for more. Good TV is made up of
quick shots which carry the viewer along in their wake.
Having worked hard on your introduction, you must now
carefully prepare the remainder of the talk so that not one
insomniac is healed!

Use humour—wisely

Back in 1976, many Americans considered Jimmy Carter
an unlikely candidate for president of the United States.
He surprised a great many people when he did win the race
for the world's most powerful political office. How did he
do it?

For one thing, he knew how to speak to people in a
way they could relate to, about things which concerned
them at the time. In the early months of his campaign, Mr
Carter would nearly always begin his speech with these
words: 'I'm Jimmy Carter. I come from a small town in
the south; I'm a farmer, a churchgoer and a family man. I
live with my wife Rosalynn and my young daughter Amy.

I served in the navy and I was a nuclear engineer. I was governor of Georgia.'

In just a few lines, Jimmy Carter had summed up all of his qualifications for high office and had pointed to all the qualities most Americans would want in their president. He did it in such a way that they felt they could trust him. In short, he had learned the art of building bridges with his audience.

Never underestimate the importance of bridge-building. For a preacher it can mean the difference between a dismal, hope-the-ground-opens-up-and-swallows-me-alive talk and a screaming three-laps-around-the-carpark success story!

There are many ways to build a bridge of trust and interest with an audience. One way you can do it is to use language.

When American president John F. Kennedy stood before the Berlin Wall in June 1963, he took a powerful visual image and added a gripping verbal image. 'Today in the world of freedom,' he said, 'the proudest boast is: *Ich bin ein Berliner.*' He used the German language to build a bridge of communication with his audience. It opened the hearts and minds of the people to hear what he had to say.

Humour is another great way of building these important talk-links with people. It helps to attract and hold the attention of your hearers. Once the bridge is up you can pass across it with the message. Sadly, the place of humour is misunderstood by all but the very best modern preachers.

Some of the best communicators in the world today are successful comedians, humorists or comic actors. Before you know it you're not just laughing at them but at human beings generally and, what's more interesting, at yourself. Once you laugh at yourself it's not so hard to see that you're imperfect and that you need to change. That's the point at which you're ready to change and grow.

Laughter is good for you. According to medical authorities, six minutes of belly laughter a day can help keep blood pressure and heart problems at bay. It can also help our moods. When people can laugh at the subject of their neuroses they are halfway towards solutions. Doctors say we are even better off when we can laugh at ourselves instead of others.[7]

Laughter is helpful in communication because it can relax people and disarm their preconceived ideas about a speaker or subject. Laughter makes people vulnerable and open to the message.

Humour, used wisely and under the inspiration of the Holy Spirit, is not irreverent. Far from it. God definitely has a sense of humour. (If you don't believe me, check out some of the people He's made!) When God came as a man to Planet Earth some killjoys accused Him of going to too many parties (Matt. 11:19). I once heard a so-called expert on the life of Jesus claim that He did not smile a great deal, that He 'wept . . . and wept . . . and wept'. This man made Jesus sound like a perpetual wet blanket. But that's not the Jesus of the Gospels. Jesus was always doing great works for people. Think about it: if you could heal the blind, the deaf and the leper and raise people from the dead, wouldn't you smile now and again?

If you've ever worked with little kids you will know that it's impossible to bore them for long—if you're not interesting they just leave or switch off. Study Jesus' life and you'll see that He was often surrounded by children.

7. 'If a Joke Fails', *The Age*, April 11, 1992.

They loved to climb up on His knee and listen to His stories. 'Uncle Jesus' they might have called Him—He was a lot of fun to be with.

G. K. Chesterton has suggested that God Himself has more than a little of the playful child in Him. (Perhaps that's why we need to become like children to enter His kingdom.) Chesterton wondered whether God didn't create a flower and then think: 'That's great, let's do it again!' He just went on creating things because He got such a kick out of it all. At the end of creation He looked at all He had made and saw that it was 'very good' or, more literally, 'the best it could be' (Gen. 1:31). God is not dull and humourless.

Sometimes Jesus said things which even today appear quite comical—though they were said to make a serious point. He often used a form of speech known as 'hyperbole'—a form often used by humorists today.

Hyperbole is a deliberate exaggeration used to make a point. An example of this is Jesus' statement: 'Why do you notice the little piece of dust in your friend's eye, but you don't notice the big piece of wood in your own eye?' (Matt. 7:3). Another is the line: 'You [Pharisees] are like a person who picks a fly out of a drink and then swallows a camel!' (Matt. 23:24).

I can see a smile on the faces of the disciples every now and then as Jesus aimed such little torpedoes at obstinate religious leaders. Much of our humour today uses deliberate exaggeration as Jesus did. Notice though that it is only funny when the audience recognises the exaggeration. Any other type of exaggeration is no more than lying—storytellers take note.

Jesus was *not* a comedian, but He did know how to use humour to make a point which would stick in people's minds. I'm not sure that any Christian preacher should be a comedian—humorist is a better word for us I think. When you're a comedian you're expected always to be funny. You get a reputation and you're tied to it, you're bound to being funny. A humorist is a speaker who can use humour as a servant without letting it take over. He or she is free to explore the creative possibilities of humour without the pressure to perform. In preaching, humour should always tickle the brain bone as well as the funny bone. Telling jokes for the sake of it is not only an insult to your audience, it also represents a compromise of your calling.

There are three sources of humour. One is the 'humour lending library'—borrowed stories or funny lines which are woven into your message. The second is 'retread humour'—tearing an old story apart and making it funny. Thirdly, there's original humour. Most funny stories are a combination of these.

There are a thousand sources of good humour all around us. In many ways, being a little funny is just about keeping your eyes and ears open. You can start by keeping files of funny stories and cartoons from newspapers and magazines. Bookshops are full of books on witticisms and quotes for public speakers. You can keep an eye on the good ol' *Readers Digest* for inspiration too. If you've used something before and it was funny, why not rewrite and fit it into a new story?

Humour's everywhere—there's a lot of it going around. But what is it that makes a thing funny? How does humour work? Here are a few observations:

Humour is a kind of trickery. Magicians amaze people with their sleight of hand. The first time you see a rabbit pulled out of a hat you think, 'Wow! I didn't expect that!' That's what humour does—it sets you up for a misunderstanding so that you expect one thing and get another.

An illustration might help. This short speech was given by a newly elected politician on the night of his victory party:

> I wish I could thank each and every one of you personally for helping me win this election. I wish I could thank all of you one at a time and shake you by the hand. Obviously, that would be ridiculous . . . because many of you were no help whatsoever.

You might have expected him to say: 'Obviously, that would take too long . . . '. Instead he hits you with the unexpected: ' . . . some of you were no help whatsoever!' The surprise is what makes it funny.

Humour is playfully aggressive. I recently stood up before an audience and said: 'It's great to be in the best church in the country. You think I know the way to all the churches, don't you? . . . I do!'

The people laughed because this gentle joke was on them. Humour has a way of playfully bringing out life's little embarrassments, but this is where discretion is needed. For a thing to be funny, it has to be fun. It can't get irreverent or too personal. It must be soft enough to be fun but hard enough to be funny—a type of soft hammer wrapped in velvet.

If you're not very careful you can come across looking like a real bully—a good way to get yourself invited to a lynching party! If the speaker in the example above had finished with, ' . . . because some of you are absolutely *useless*!' his line would not have been funny.

Humour is about timing and proportion. Our friendly politician would not have been so humorous if he jumped to the punch-line (the rabbit in the hat) too quickly:

> I wish I could thank all of you for helping me win this election. Obviously I can't—some of you were no help whatsoever.

Instead, he wisely draws out the whole thing—he really butters the people up, so that the punch is so much more surprising. The timing's important too. Just that little pause before the last few words is what makes or breaks his humour. This is largely natural, but it can be learned and developed with practice.

Humour is about being sensitive. There are times in a message when it's best to avoid humour altogether. It can so easily take away from a serious point you want to make, or from something prophetic the Lord wants to say through you.

Humour is about being confident. It's difficult to be funny if you're meekly trying to hedge around an issue. If something is humorous, you've got to come right out with it, you can't be too tentative. Humour involves speaking with a kind of relaxed authority, knowing that you'll make people laugh. Confidence grows with experience.

Humour is about being vulnerable. The most effective humour you can use in public speaking is based on things which have happened to you personally. People relate to

speakers who know how to laugh at themselves, without
putting themselves down in the process.

When I was at school I hated Physical Education
('Phys. Ed.' for short), for two reasons: first of all because
we had to wear sports uniform. I was a little on the skinny
side—when I wore shorts the police would arrest me for
having no visible means of support. I'd run onto the football field looking like something out of *Revenge of the
Nerds 3*.

The other reason I hated sports lessons was that we
had to endure an ancient tribal ritual called 'Choosing
Teams'—perhaps you've heard of it, or worse still, been
through it! There were two groups of boys in my school:
the fast developers and the slow developers. The fast
developers bulked out overnight—they went home one day
looking like PeeWee Herman and came back looking like
Arnold Stationwagon. Their voices dropped overnight and
they were shaving at the age of twelve—of course, some of
their mothers had beards too!

The slow developers, of which I was one, went home
one day looking like PeeWee Herman and came back the
next looking like Roger Rabbit! My voice didn't change
until I was sixteen: it was so up and down I sounded like a
yodeller. Choosing teams consisted of the teachers
appointing two of the biggest fast developers to become
captains who would choose their teams from the rest of us
plebs. It always ended the same way. Me and my friends,
proud members of the school chess team, were on the end
of the line, left until last.

There's more to this story than I can relate here and I
would always incorporate visual humour with it. Most
people, young and old, relate to this uncomfortable
situation. While they're laughing at human nature, they're

thinking about it. While they're thinking about it, they're open to change and that's when I close in for the kill!

Remember: humour is only a means to an end—it is a good servant but a poor master. Use it wisely. Make sure it illustrates some worthwhile point and learn how to move your audience from laughter to an intelligent response to a real challenge.

Develop storytelling skills

It was November 1963 and broadcaster Richard Dimbleby offered the following as part of his report on the funeral of John F. Kennedy:

> And so outside to the sunshine, where the bearer party, some of them coloured servicemen, drawn from all the services, proudly, reverently and carefully, bear their dead president and commander-in-chief down the steep steps, back to the gun carriage which waits for them at the bottom . . . Mrs Kennedy, the children, the mourners follow down the steps behind.[8]

These are the thoughts of not just a good reporter, but a very good storyteller. He is doing more than relating events, he is painting visual images in his hearers' minds. He is carrying them to the scene via the age-old art of vivid storytelling.

Most of the great preachers in history have been skilful storytellers. Jesus, of course, was the ultimate exponent of the storytelling craft. He knew how to take everyday events in the lives of real people and turn them

---

8. Peter Thompson, *The Secrets of the Great Communicators* (ABC Books, 1992). p. 39.

into powerful object lessons which are not easily forgotten. Had Jesus not been such an awesome storyteller His early disciples might have had less success in remembering what He taught, and the Gospels might never have been written.

What can we learn from Jesus about storytelling? For a start, Jesus' stories made you think. Jesus was not in the habit of giving His stories titles—scholars did that in more modern times. The Lord did not start with something like: 'Did you hear the one about the prodigal son?' He simply told the story and left you to think about what it meant to you. Jesus didn't often explain His stories either. At times he'd expound a little more for the benefit of His disciples, but even that was brief and to the point. Jesus knew that, unless we're forced to think about an idea for ourselves, we'll never really own it and make it a part of our lives.

He also knew that some of his hearers had 'ears to hear' (Mark 4:23 KJV) what the Spirit of God was saying. Others wouldn't really hear—that is with the ear of the heart, in a way which would change their actions. Those people wouldn't benefit from further explanation anyway.

Our stories should not be so complex that people can't see the point if they're really listening and open.

Reading Jesus' stories you'll also find that, while they weren't sensationalised to manipulate people's feelings, they were gripping. The story we call 'The Good Samaritan' is an example (Luke 10:25–37). Who could help but feel empathy and sympathy for the broken man by the side of the road—and anger towards those who passed him by? Even reading the story now, you find yourself imagining you're there watching it all happen, or taking part as one of the characters. And what about the story of Dives the rich man and the beggar Lazarus (Luke 16:19–31)? Our stories should be told in a way which gets people emotionally involved. It must be said too, that Jesus stories were emotive for other people because they moved *Him*! He was really stirred up about the injustice of Lazarus' situation and that's the primary reason He could speak with authority—He *felt* what He was saying, deeply and sincerely.

There are so many sources for good stories. Phil Pringle tells us there are five types of stories available to us: personal testimonies, fantasy stories (parables you've made up), Bible stories, testimonies from the lives of others and humorous stories.[9] Modern writers such as Frank Peretti are using fantasy stories to great effect in getting across a message.

Myths are a legitimate form of communication too. C. S. Lewis used these to great effect in books like *Perelandra* and *Out of the Silent Planet*. Myths 'contain universal truth presented in a solemn picture or story form to help our understanding'.[10]

If you can't find draw good stories from your own life experience, start reading biographies and human interest stories in weekend newspapers. There's a million stories all around you.

The stories of Jesus were also repeated. Many commentators agree that His stories, or at least some of them, were probably retold on a number of occasions in different places. Repetition causes the hearers to get the point and have it stick in their minds for good. From the speaker's point of view a story gets better with the retelling. We share it more effectively the more often we use it. Even

9. Phil Pringle, *Faith* (Seam of Gold, 1991), p. 50.

10. Anne Arnot, *The Secret Country of C. S. Lewis* (Lakeland, 1974), p. 99.

rehearsing it in private can help us deliver it with maximum effect.

Stories are useful because they throw light upon a subject. This is what the word 'illustration' literally means. Well-chosen and well-constructed stories serve as windows into ideas you want to communicate. Again, stories should be the servant of preaching and never the master—they must not be used just for the sake of it. There must be some purpose, some goal you want to reach in the sharing of any story. Otherwise, it's just excess baggage and you won't get off the ground while you hold on to it.

Get to the point

One American president, Franklin D. Roosevelt, gave some excellent advice to all speakers: 'Be sincere, be brief and be seated.'

Sir Winston Churchill was asked about why he spoke in such simple terms. 'I like short words,' he replied. So do most audiences—they want short words and short speeches. They don't want to be impressed with your vocabulary—they want to be immersed in your ideas and your convictions. They want to leave wanting more, not hating what they got.

Don't waste precious time and audience attention by waffling on about side-issues, or telling stories which have no bearing on your main subject. Don't go off on tangents. It's far better to speak for 10 minutes and say something worth remembering than to go on for 45 minutes and bore even the walls! As a general rule, if you can't say what you need to in around 20 to 30 minutes, you don't deserve to be speaking.

One of the most powerful messages I ever heard went like this:

Some men die from shrapnel,
Some men die in pain;
But most men die inch by inch,
Playing little games.

What a gutsy little paragraph! It is economical with words but absolutely loaded with emotion and a message to make you think. Here's another little line which has stuck in the minds of a generation:

Ask not what your country can do for you. Ask what you can do for your country.

John F. Kennedy

Keep it simple!

Use dynamics

Musicians know all about the importance of dynamics. Without variety of expression, soft and loud or fast and slow, a piece of music becomes monotonous. There needs to be 'space' and variety in music—opportunity for the ear to distinguish the sounds and moods and thus keep the hearer interested. It's the same with preaching, where two types of dynamic need to be employed.

I was born into a third-generation Christian home. We went to two church services every Sunday, so I've seen more than a few preachers in action. Some of them would bore me to tears because they spoke as if they were on Valium—so laid back they almost fell over. I'd wake up just as they were leaving. Others would spend 40 minutes bellowing out some drivel at the tops of their voices, as if they were John Wesley preaching to 20,000 people in an open field instead of 50 people in a weatherboard chapel.

You'd think all that yelling would have kept me on the edge of my seat. Instead, it had exactly the same effect as the timid style—I fell asleep or drifted off into dreamland. My mind simply refused to stay tuned when someone was using me for wind-tunnel testing!

In good preaching, as in fine music, there will always be points of soft and loud, or oral dynamics. Variety produces interest. You don't need to shout at people for half an hour to make your point. TV doesn't grab them that way. By the same token you can't afford to preach as if you're scared to open your mouth for fear of putting your foot in it! Confidence is essential. But holding the attention of an audience will require that you mix up the loud and the not-so-loud, that you have sections where everything's going at once—arms, legs, face, voice—and others where there's time to pause and consider. Dynamics allow people opportunity to assimilate what you're saying.

When you're starting out as a public speaker, it might help to practise some of your delivery in private, making a mental note of points which need to be emphasised with increased volume and others which need a softer touch. It may also help to listen to a tape of yourself preaching or to get a trusted (and not too negative) friend to give feedback on your performance. It may frighten you when first you hear your own voice, but don't despair—you *can* improve!

Then there's the visual side of our speaking. I've seen preachers who, at the climax of their message, invite you to come to Christ with their words, but their actions suggest you shouldn't come. They're moving backwards while they speak, or frowning, or pointing threateningly at you as if to drive you back. Body language reveals a great deal about a speaker. It is an important, though unconscious, part of his or her delivery. We need dynamics here too—variety in our movement and gestures. We need to study the way we move in front of people so that we don't betray our words with contradictory movements. Why not get someone to video your next public talk so that you can watch for overly repetitive movements or those which distract from your message?

I remember my first tentative attempts at speaking to a crowd. I was as nervous as a dog at a flea circus. One thing which helped me get through it all was deliberately smiling at people as I spoke. Smiling helps the audience relax with you and helps you feel less intimidated by them. It's a great place to start to improve your visual effect.

Clothing is another part of visual communication. Wearing a tie and three-piece suit won't make you a lot of friends if you're addressing a school assembly. Turning up to speak at a Sunday morning church service dressed in slashed jeans, a T-shirt and a Spurs cap won't go down too well either. Dress in a way that's appropriate to the occasion, so that people are not distracted from the message. Don't let little things about you divert people's attention from the important things you're teaching about Christ.

Use language with skill

I'm one of those musicians who's not very good at reading music—it all looks like so many golf sticks to me. I'd never have made it as a composer in the eighteenth century before multi-track recording was invented. I do, however, know the basic laws of music theory—the conventions which rule the way notes and chords are put together in a meaningful way. Without the laws of music,

it all becomes noise. Without road laws there'd be more
accidents; without the laws of music there'd be more
earaches.

And now, I have much pleasure in introducing
brother Fred Dork, who's going to minister God's word.
Thank you brother Dork . . .

> 'Well . . . er . . . hello. It's . . . um . . . good to see
> yuz all 'ere . . . um . . . I'm gunna learn yuz all how
> to . . . um . . . er . . . talk proper when yu
> witness . . . '

A great start isn't it? Riveting stuff! Sadly, there are
a lot of preachers today who've never learned how to
respect language and put words together well. Language is
a preacher's weapon. Sloppy and lazy grammar is an insult
to the hearer. If your language skills get rusty, don't be
surprised if your barrel's bent and you shoot around cor-
ners. Members of an audience expect public speakers to
treat language with respect and to know more about its use
than they do.

There are a couple of traps you should avoid. Read
the following and see if it rings a proverbial bell:

> Mary was the legal owner of one diminutive poten-
> tial sheep, whose haliberments were as lacking in
> colour as congealed atmospheric vapour. Wherever
> the ultimate destination of Mary's peregrinations the
> pre-pubescent sheep was certain to accompany her.

> The aforesaid miniature animal accompanied Mary
> to her place of learning one post-nocturnal period
> which was in clear breach of the stated regulations

of that body. This circumstance was the cause of exceeding merriment among the junior homo-sapiens.

'What was *that*?!' you're shrieking! Surely you recognise *Mary had a Little Lamb*? No? Perhaps that's because it was written the way some preachers speak—with a bad case of ingrown tongue. Don't be afraid to express yourself in simple terms. No one will accuse you of being simple-minded.

There are three levels of communication. There are big ideas expressed with small words. There are small ideas shared in small words. Then there are *big* ideas poured into *small* words—that's real communication!

Even slang, which is so much a part of youth culture, has to be used carefully by the preacher. Young people can tell straight off if we're using words we're not familiar with, or throwing in phrases we've never used before. (People have inbuilt plastic detectors!) Besides, it's too easy to get out of touch with the current lingo—better to be cautious. Try something like this with a group of 90s teenagers:

> OK all you cool cats out there in groove-land! It's a real gas to be with you all—I really dig it, like. Let me lay a heavy thing on you man. It's a real trip to be a Jesus person—I mean, like, a real natural high.

You're dead meat, dude!

If you're not confident with the words you use and the construction of sentences, you can improve in a number of ways. Reading is a great way to get ahead. Read books not just for content but for style. Find writers who express themselves in unique and interesting ways and soak in the way they use language. Listening to recordings of good speakers is another path to improvement. Invest in some cassettes of well-known preachers. Then there's learning to write well. Lifting your writing skills through night-school courses and the like will increase your confidence with words.

Speak with passion

A great speaker's feelings of conviction are the dominant message. Their feelings are never cool . . . audiences often forget what is said but they can always remember how it was said.[11]

No matter who the audience or what the subject, your job as a speaker is to mobilise an emotional response. As one advertising authority has put it: 'You've got to arouse people.'[12] You must arouse feelings and then focus that emotion towards some worthwhile purpose.

The ancient Greeks established a long tradition in the art of oratory. They even established a set of rules to govern effective speech. For the Greeks there were three elements in a speech. There was *ethos*, the credibility of the speaker. There was *logos*, the words used, the content of the speech. Finally there was *pathos*, the emotional bridge which was built between the speaker and the hearer.

Modern advertising agencies understand the place of *pathos* in getting their message across. In the electronic media in particular, they try to arouse anger, irritation,

11. Peter Thompson, op. cit. p. 11.

12. Quoted, ibid. p. 28.

sorrow, conflict—whatever it takes to motivate you to buy!

Jesus was a passionate speaker and person. Many times Scripture tells of His compassion for people around Him, a love He was not ashamed to show (Matt. 9:36). Sadly, people today often picture God as a dispassionate Being who is unmoved by our traumas, partly because we've made Him look ineffectual by the way we talk about Him. We've fed our world a pasty-faced, limp-wristed, Father Mulcahy (of M*A*S*H fame) picture of God. If we had a little more passion when we spoke, people might start to get the right idea. We've gone too much for the head and not enough for the heart!

When we preach, the impact of what we say is greatly affected by the way we say it. Psychologists speak about a concept known as 'anchoring'. The idea is that the words we speak to each other are more powerful when they're combined with strong non-verbal signals. Our words literally carry more weight as a result of—they're 'anchored' in—our actions.

You should speak on things about which you have strong feelings because feelings make a more lasting impression than facts on their own. That's why the best stories you can tell will be about things which have happened to you. Don't be too afraid to use the word 'I'— people actually like frankness. Of course, what we share should be accurate, but the medium is the message— people will base their responses on what they think is your own reaction to what you're teaching them. If you're not moved, neither will they be.

You should know the subject so well, through your preparation and study, that it becomes a part of you. Developing a passion both for the people you address and for your subject will help you speak authentically. You will be real.

Speak with integrity

There's a great deal of talk in some church circles about 'anointing' and how preachers need to be 'anointed by the Holy Spirit'. But what *is* this thing we call anointing?

Perhaps we should start with what it is not. People are often said to be anointed in their ministries if they can move others emotionally. So, when there's a charismatic speaker with a swag of heart-gripping stories, people know he or she is anointed. Real anointing, however, is more than emotion or atmosphere. Not everyone who can move a crowd has anything of life-giving substance to say. Over the years, the church has heard from too many people who were not really anointed—they were just talented and knew how to 'work the crowd'. Some of the most effective speakers the church has seen have not been good 'performers' at all.

We can't measure anointing by whether we feel good about someone's ministry. I have no right to say, for example, that because I happen to enjoy country music a Christian is more anointed if he or she plays country than if they're into rock. Anointing is more substantial than that.

Anointing is actually the manifest presence of God. It is God showing Himself to us. Let me illustrate that. If we're in a meeting and we see a person miraculously healed, we know that God is saying, 'Hey, I'm here.' If we hear a word or prophecy and know it is accurate, that's God tapping us on the shoulder and saying, 'I'm here.' God loves to display for us His love and power in response to human need.

The last phrase is important. God's anointing does

not come through some human whim—you and I can't simply turn it on to have some fun. God only ever reveals Himself for a reason, to meet a need. His presence with us will always accomplish something specific. If a physical healing is what's needed, the Lord won't give a word of prophecy, or vice versa.

Sometimes anointing gives us the 'warm fuzzies'. It comforts and encourages us and makes our spirits soar. At other times, anointing comes as conviction—it unsettles us and pulls the rug out from under our feet. Feelings of conviction are just as much part of anointing as are feelings of elation.

Ultimately it is God who allows people to function in certain aspects of His anointing. Some Christians are very good at praying for the sick and seeing them healed. Others are gifted at preaching apologetically. Some are able to lead large groups in worship. We are each anointed for different things and that much is God's business. But we do have some say in how we carry that anointing. On many occasions people who started out with a great ministry have ended their lives in misery. They did not learn to match the other areas of their lives with their area of gift. They assumed that their gifts were enough.

Whilst none of us can really choose in what areas God might want to anoint us—to manifest His power through us—we can hinder that anointing through our lack of preparation for ministry and our disregard for issues of personal integrity.

Here's what one old preacher said about this:

[There is a kind of preacher] who has never been in the hands of God like clay in the hands of the potter. He has been busy about the sermon, its thought, its finish . . . but the deep things of God have never been sought, studied, fathomed, experienced by him. He has never . . . had his life renewed, his heart touched, purged, inflamed by the live coal from God's altar.

Repeat yourself . . . repeat yourself

Psychologists tell us that we can easily recall a new idea only when we've heard it about six times. When preaching you should repeat your basic premise or idea many times throughout the message. Consider this little extract from a speech by Winston Churchill, given just before the crucial Battle of Britain:

> We shall fight in France. We shall fight on the seas and oceans. We shall fight with growing confidence and growing strength in the air. We shall defend our island, whatever the cost may be. We shall fight on the beaches. We shall fight in the fields and in the streets. We shall fight in the hills. We shall never surrender.

People certainly got the message—we shall fight! Of course, it's not always healthy to be so obvious in your repetition of ideas. You will need to look for creative ways to express them, so that you don't bore people by restating them in the same words each time. Telling stories is a great way of subtly restating an idea.

Don't hide!

At one leaders' conference, I was expected to speak from behind a pulpit which resembled the front of a Mercedes semitrailer. The thing was so huge you could bungee-

110

jump from the top of it! You could have rented it out for low-cost family housing. Needless to say, I asked them to move the thing whenever it was my turn to speak. How can you involve people in what you're saying when you're peering out from behind a two-ton lectern?

In fact, even small pulpits can be more of a hindrance than a help. You should only use them if you really need to consult your notes, and then only sparingly. You should definitely not spend your entire time standing on the spot, afraid to venture out from behind a piece of furniture. You'll do yourself—and your audience—a great service, if you learn not to rely too heavily on written notes. Notes usually require somewhere to sit and that can be distracting for everyone concerned.

More on that in the next section. Read on, intrepid warrior . . .

5

Prepare or Die!!

'Well, it's great to be here speaking to you today. I didn't have a thing prepared for today's meeting—I wanted to let the Spirit carry me along. As I was sitting here during the worship time, I was flicking through my Bible when a Scripture just leaped out and grabbed me by the throat! Now I know what God wants me to share with you . . . (I think).'

Ever heard anything like that? Some preachers don't seem to believe in preparation. They stand up before a crowd, smile, close their eyes and hope for the best. Then they display their ignorance for an hour by jumping from one irrelevant subject to another, adding to the already significant 'word-pollution' in our atmosphere.

Those preachers may cop out by telling you they're relying on God's anointing. In the last chapter we saw that anointing is God getting our attention and that God's anointing of my ministry will be affected by how I live my life in private. How much God can work with and through me when I speak will also be tied to my behind-the-scenes preparation—my study, prayer and meditation. Every one of us must look (into our subject and our hearts) before we leap (into the pulpit)! There is simply no way you can reap if you haven't sown—there ain't no shortcuts, people.

My Brain Hurts . . .

> There are two kinds of preacher: one who has some-
> thing to say and the other who has to say something.
>
> Unknown

Ever suffered from brain drain? You know, your mind
feels as if it's got backache—it just wants to take a long
bath and go to bed. That's how it can feel when you're
looking for something to speak on. You want to bring
something fresh, something anointed, something which
will dazzle the audience and shake the city! But what are
you going to talk about?

Some novelists claim that over thirty per cent of their
success is in the original idea for the story. For preachers it
might be closer to fifty per cent. You simply can't get
away with having nothing much to say.

So where do the ideas come from? I think there are
several sources.

The Bible is the most obvious. Preaching is about
making the God of the Bible real to us, in our own daily
concerns and needs.

When you read the Bible it helps to have a notebook
nearby. For me, more good ideas, more real revelations,
come from regular systematic Bible reading than from
irregular marathon, 'hit the books' sessions. Try to relax
when you read—it's hard to hear from heaven when you're
tensed up.

Make a commitment to read first and study later. By
that I mean don't allow time with God's word to become
too complicated, cluttered. Some well-known preachers
make reading the Bible, and praying, seem so difficult.

They tell you that unless you buy their 25-set cassette series on reading the Word, you'll never really understand what you're doing. If you don't read their 13-in-the-set manuals you'll never tackle prayer. Somehow, Jesus managed to teach us to pray in around nine lines! Don't let anyone make these things seem too complex for you.

It's a good idea to relax whenever you read the Bible. At times, God can't get through to us because we're too tense. Find somewhere relatively quiet if you can and just 'chill out' with the Lord. You shouldn't expect an earth-shattering discovery every time you read your Bible. Sometimes it is the simple things which change our lives. We need those to help us understand the real 'off the wall' revelations when they occur.

It's a good idea to carry a small Bible or Testament with you in your car, handbag or briefcase, so you can 'fill up' whenever the personal tank gets low.

Some misguided people have told me that it's 'wrong to read the Bible just for sermon material'. It's not—if you're willing to live what you preach!

Your studies on current social issues will often suggest themes too. These may be drawn from your research reading or they may come out of personal counselling. If you're involved in pastoral work, you'll sometimes find that numbers of people in your care are facing the same pressures all at the one time. You may need to teach on those areas of need, without making anyone feel that you're preaching 'at' them.

Ideas may also come through listening to other speakers, or reading Christian literature. Try to read a really challenging or helpful book more than once and bring something home from every leadership conference you attend. Hey, it's not wrong to borrow ideas if they're good ones. After all, there's 'nothing new under the sun' (Eccles. 1:9 NIV).

Some of the best messages you'll ever preach will be those based upon the dealings of God in your own life. They're powerful because you don't have to work to make them a part of you. You can launch forth with passion and with empathy because you've been there and done that. Of course, you need to base your teaching on solid Bible foundations, not just experiences.

I've found that in my daily walk with God, certain themes have arisen over time. Concepts have developed slowly within me, coming only gradually to maturity. I end up preaching on those issues for quite a long period— as God deepens my understanding of them, my teaching also deepens and broadens. In many ways it is far better to seek God for that kind of 'big picture' concept, rather than just a one-off idea here and there. There's no reason why you should not preach on one very personalised subject many times—provided you do it in different ways each time.

What Do I Do Now?

OK, so the ideas are flowing and you're prepared to put in the study time required of a good speaker. Well done. So where to from here? Now it's time to get those ideas down on paper, *then to get them into you!*

We've already noted that involvement is the name of the game when you're speaking in public. One of the simplest ways of breaking the chain of communication between you and your audience is constantly to be diverting your eyes away from them to read lengthy sections of notes. Notes should really be more of an aid to you before you get in front of the group than when you're speaking.

Most of us are using our memories, our powers of recall, at far below their capacity. We have simply never developed a confidence in our ability to call up information when we need it. As a result we bind ourselves to our notes, afraid to venture too far from the 'safe water' around the precious pulpit.

Preachers who do not need to rely heavily on notes have a great weapon in their arsenal—the eyeball. Those preachers are able to make each member of a crowd feel as if they could be talking just to him or her. In TV land autocues were invented to save newsreaders from looking at their notes rather than into the camera. Producers felt that people would trust their TV presenters more if they had what looked like eye contact—it's hard to trust someone who keeps looking away when they're talking to you. If eye contact is important to news reporters, it is even more essential to Good News reporters.

The development of the memory not only makes us more accessible to our audience, it also helps us to speak with more passion. The message becomes so much a part of us that it flows out with conviction. We do not need to break the stream of words to consult our notes every few minutes.

How can I prepare for maximum effectiveness and minimum notes? Here's a little strategy I use myself:

Stage 1: Do your reading
Don't be lazy. Collect as much information as you reasonably can on the subject or text at hand. Read up on your cross-references, get into the biographies, gather informa-

tion and facts, making notes as you go. Spread your notes and all your key reference materials out on your desk so that the whole mass of clay is in front of you, ready to be sculpted by the master (that's you).

Stage 2: Do your first draft

Take out a large sheet of paper—or several smaller ones— and begin to jot down all your major ideas, themes, facts and illustrations. Just write quickly as the ideas flow. Connect things up with arrows, draw little pictures, do whatever comes naturally. Take a pit stop every now and again to pray and meditate, then get back to it.

This sheet might look like hieroglyphics to any other human being—it doesn't matter, as you're the only one who needs to read it. Sometimes your desk will look like an explosion in a papermill when you've finished—books and reference materials spread everywhere. That's OK. This is just the initial 'schematic design' stage.

Stage 3: Stop and clear the desk

You need to stop somewhere, even if you feel you could go on scribbling for ever. Clear the desk. Start to organise your initial ideas into a more logical format, editing out whatever is unnecessary to the message (even if it is interesting). Go over your first page with a coloured pen, marking sections with consecutive numbers to show where they should fit in the sequence of things.

Stage 4: Start sculpting

This is where it gets interesting. There are basically three stages in a good message, as there are in an essay: introduction, development (or defence) and conclusion. The first stage involves giving a taste of your major theme while, as we've already noted, getting your audience emotionally hooked before they're aware of it.

The second stage is where you expand on your introductory remarks, breaking your major theme or text down into smaller sub-themes or ideas and illustrating these ideas with stories, humour and the like. You must always seek to show people how these truths affect their lives.

In the final stage in the message, the conclusion, you are wrapping up—restating the major themes and challenging people to act upon what they've heard.

Take out a new sheet of paper and start rewriting the ideas you've sketched out in a more logical order, based around these three stages. Expand on them as you go, adding illustrative material—stories, humour and so on—to add impact. That's it for stage four—now it gets interesting.

Stage 5: Final draft

Now take your second draft notes and rewrite them one more time. But this time speak as you write—that is, say what you've written before you rewrite it for the final time. This will help you to write statements the way you say them. You see, most of us will write differently from the way we speak; the flow of language is different when we speak. So you need to store statements in your memory in the way that they'll be spoken. Otherwise your delivery will be constantly slowed down as your brain translates from written word to spoken word.

Stage 6: Turn your memory on

Once you've written this final draft go over it again and again, memorising one section at a time. The brain tends to connect our thoughts. Picture the process as being like chains of separate concepts all strung together. If the links of the chain are made strong by continual use, one idea will automatically lead to the next one in the chain. Memorising one point after another will strengthen the chain of ideas so that as soon as you speak out the first main point, the next one will come to mind. Don't write your final draft in long hand. Put down major headings followed by illustrations and a few texts under each.

This may all seem like too much hard work, but it's the speakers who've worked hardest who can make it look easy!

Some people have trained their memory to the point where they don't need notes before them when they speak. Perhaps you're not that confident yet. In that case it's better to use notes than to ramble. Why not put your thoughts down on small cards which will fit easily into your palm? With these you will be able to read the main points quickly at a glance. Or you might slip a small sheet of notes inside your open Bible. In either case, make sure your notes are brief and cover only the major points. That will force you to rely at least a little on your recall.

Be creative
I wonder what Jesus would have done if He'd had modern communications technology at His disposal. I think He might have seen its value and used it with great effect. Over the centuries great preachers have used visual aids to reinforce their message. Jesus did it: He used lilies, sparrows, fig trees and much more. Today's technology makes it even easier for us to call up images which will reinforce a message.

Alongside the plain old blackboard we can now tap into video and computer images, slide projection, drama set to recorded music, programmable keyboards with built-in sound effects and a host of other media. Soon we'll have 'artificial reality' computer imaging and holograms.

Why should God's preachers be afraid to use all this for His glory? We must remember that the message is the primary thing and everything else is there to serve the message. Also, nothing will ever replace the anointing of the Spirit. But we should use every creative means available to us to make the message, in the words of Nat King Cole, 'unforgettable . . . '

Don't be nervous about being nervous!
'Tomorrow night,' said Mark Twain, America's immortal writer, 'I appear for the first time before a Boston audience—four thousand critics!'

Twain summed up how we often feel before facing the madding crowd. Everybody gets nervous! Some people *look* cooler than a London winter, but that's because they've learned to channel their nervous energy (or *lie* well!).

I find that nerves actually set me up to speak with more feeling. There was a time when my nerves tied me up in knots so that I couldn't function well at all, but I've learned a few things since then. One of the most effective ways I've discovered for dealing with nerves is to sit down and pray my way through a message before I go on. I actually ask the Lord's help to minister in each of the areas I will cover, going from one point to the next. It's a great way to get mentally prepared while you're tuning up spiritually. But I make sure it's quiet prayer, so that I don't wear out the vocal chords.

Simple breathing exercises can also help. Try breathing in while you count slowly to ten, making sure that your diaphragm and not your chest is moving. Then exhale the same way. Do this a few times and it will help you to relax, without losing momentum.

It's helpful to picture in your imagination a good outcome—to 'see' people looking interested, appreciating your message. Spend time thanking the Lord for what He will do, in advance. Nerves don't have to be so terrifying.

Rely on the Holy Spirit

It is not the preacher but the Spirit of God who convicts of sin, righteousness and judgement to come (John 16:8). He comes to guide people into all truth (John 16:13). Some preachers put together their own thoughts and opinions and then flippantly hope the Holy Spirit will endorse and support what they have to say. We must treat the Spirit of God with more respect than this. We are His vessels, not He ours. Include the Holy Spirit in every aspect of your preparation—talk to Him constantly and have your ears open for His direction, encouragement or loving rebuke.

The Levis Test ...

Ever seen a TV commercial for Levi 501s? (They're jeans, if you didn't know.) How do Mr Strauss and Co. attract the youth market to their product? Well, they film a wire coathanger with a pair of said jeans draped over it, don't they? Wrong. They bring out some gorgeous babe or some multi-muscled male who just happens to be wearing the 501s and looking awesome! Heads turn as the proud wearer glides by in style. Members of the opposite sex are turned on by these threads. Life is good if you wear Levis.

TV commercials feature models who look like all our

dreams come true. They try to convince you that your life will be improved in certain ways if you buy this product. They demonstrate how your life might change. When we preach we should be showing people how the gospel will look when they 'wear it' in everyday life. The acid test for any message is: how has it changed people's lives?

I've spoken at hundreds of outreach rallies and concerts over the years. On one occasion a woman wrote to me after one of these saying how much she'd enjoyed and been challenged by the ministry. However, she said, wasn't it a shame there wasn't more 'real' repentance in the young people who came forward to accept Christ? How did she know? Well, there weren't many tears shed at the front.

I wrote back and graciously questioned her definition of repentance. Repenting has little to do with shedding tears. I've seen people cry until their cheeks shrink, and then go home and live tomorrow without any change for the better. Repentance is in fact a decision, a commitment to live today in a different way from the way I would if I was not a Christian. Before I met Christ, if my boss told me off I might tell him where to go! But because I'm a Christian I won't do that now. That's repentance—allowing the gospel actually to change my behaviour in specific situations.

Preaching must always be aimed at producing some kind of repentance, some change in people. Before I speak I must seek God about what kind of change He wants to see as a result of my message. How does He want people to apply what I've taught? In what practical ways can I inspire people to lay down their lives for the cause of Christ? Unless we address these questions each time we speak, we will find that our messages will become abstract and impractical. People can only see a message as a real part of their lives when they can translate it into action.

Winston Churchill left no doubt what his wartime messages to the nation were for. He called people to action, to lay down their very lives in the struggle if necessary:

> We shall fight on the beaches. We shall fight on the landing grounds. We shall fight in the fields and in the streets. We shall fight in the hills. We shall never surrender.

When they heard the Prime Minister speak, British people knew what was expected of them—everything.

When one group of ex-church kids were asked why they no longer went to church, they replied: ' . . . at church we were underchallenged.' What a sad indictment of the message we preach. People do not want an easy-fix, light-weight Christianity; they want to be challenged to reach greater heights. In fact, Dr Billy Graham has suggested that people sometimes turn to false cults because 'The cults make demands. People want a challenge. They respond to a call to hardship.'[1] It's a call we seldom make in our preaching.

There are times when we forget we are actually preaching to ordinary people. We'd like to think of our audience as being made up of spiritual giants, heroes of the faith who come to us for a weekly dose of 'deep teaching'. Most of the people who hear us preach are not great spiritual athletes. They don't know, or care, much about the Greek and Hebrew languages. They don't want an

---

1. Billy Graham, *Approaching Hoofbeats: the Four Horsemen of the Apocalypse* (Avon Books, 1983), p. 105.

education in philosophy or an essay in ethics. They're just everyday people struggling to make sense of everyday problems.

Let me suggest a few challenges which need to be featured in our preaching to 'ordinary people'. I leave it to you to put flesh on the bones:

God has a claim on our lives

We don't come to God simply because of our needs. To preach about human need alone is to centre on man and not on God. He will meet our needs, but only as we bow to His Lordship. God's first call to us is a call to repentance (see Acts 17:30).

Man is guilty, not merely helpless

Some psychiatrists are now teaching that we should return to teaching people personal responsibility for wrongdoing, instead of simply blaming it on their genes or environment. This, they say, is the way to produce hope for people. You see, if my decisions are partly responsible for my problems, then I can produce positive change by making better decisions. According to the Bible, each human being is responsible for how they respond to the situation in which they find themselves. Before God sin is not just a disease—it is a choice; and man is not merely hurting—he is in rebellion. He must undergo a fundamental change of heart.

Love is primarily a decision, not a feeling

God loves me because of an act of will, not an act of whim. His love is based upon an eternal decision to love. His love for me does not run hot and cold like the temperature of public opinion. That's the way I am commanded to love others—out of obedience to Him, not feelings of convenience for me. I'm to love by act of decision—even my enemies are to be treated with grace and mercy. I am to treat my fellow human beings not as the world does, but as they should be in the new Kingdom, where God's ways are the norm. My feelings towards people are not to be the key to my behaviour—God's commands are my foundation for action.

Holiness is not an option (or a drag!)

Every Christian is commanded to live a pure life with the help of the Holy Spirit. The prerequisite for holy living is yieldedness—abandoning myself and my wishes and rights to let Jesus do as He wants in each situation. We need to teach the young what holiness looks like in practical everyday situations: with regard to sexuality, for example, or our dealings with the law of the land, or our approach to authority structures, including parents and teachers.

Remember, preacher: holiness is not produced in people by badgering them with legalistic jargon (see Mark 7:7–8). Holiness is as much caught as taught—people learn it watching us.

The Last Shall Be First . . .

OK, so you've preached a blinder of a message. It was so good you feel like doing a victory lap around the church car park. But you haven't finished yet. You've still got to wrap the whole thing up somehow.

The conclusion is in many ways the most important part of a public talk. Yet it's often the most neglected. We should work as hard on finishing as we did on beginning. The end of the message must be carefully planned and executed. At this point people are making their decisions about whether your message will influence them.

You should draw to a close when you know people will go away wanting more. Too often speakers reach a climax, a point where people would climb Everest if that's what God wanted, only to lose all that emotional commitment by going on for another fifteen minutes.

'It's a good thing,' goes an old saying, 'for the preacher to stop preaching before the audience stops listening.' Some other wit remarked that, 'The eternal gospel doesn't need an everlasting sermon!'

There are several ways to wrap up. Sometimes it is best to finish with a moving story which will pack both an emotional punch and a challenge to action. There is nothing wrong with emotion—it's a powerful motivator. (Remember when you spent your last cent buying that special gift for your teenage girl/boyfriend?) Don't be afraid to move your audience, to carry them towards action on the back of a passionate appeal. Of course, this approach has all too often been abused. Some preachers manipulate their audiences with overly tearful or dramatised appeals, exaggerating their stories and colouring their language to pull at heart strings. They measure their success by emotion alone. Yet real success in God's eyes is not simply a matter of whether people cried, or shouted, or ran to the front: good fruit is fruit which lasts (John 15:16). A truly successful message is one which will produce a long-term effect in people's lives.

Sometimes it's better to conclude with a humorous—but thought-provoking—anecdote. This works well in an informal setting or with a secular audience. At other times you may pose a probing question and leave your audience thinking about it. Whatever method you choose, design your closing remarks for maximum results. The audience must remember what you've had to say long after they've left the building.

So, now you've finished the talk. There's one last thing to attend to. There must be adequate people follow-up after you've spoken, especially if you're asking people to respond for salvation or for further counselling on needs. Someone has to be available to answer their questions, pray with them and offer them ongoing support. These workers should be trained in the art of listening so that they hear people out before they give advice.

Not every message you preach will require a public response. Sometimes it's best to leave people thinking on what you've said, challenging them to evaluate their position before God on the issues you've raised. In those instances, you don't want to spoil the impact of your challenge by getting into loud or boisterous music at the end. Keep the tone of things at a more thoughtful level. However, when you know an immediate response is the order of the day, go for it and, please, do it well. Here are a few helpful pointers on handling public response times at the end of a message:

1. Pray about the appeal

Dr Billy Graham is one seasoned campaigner who ought to know a thing or too about giving an appeal. He has said a number of times that for him the appeal is the most strenuous and demanding part of the message, for it is here that people are facing a real spiritual battle as they prepare to make their decision. Eternal values are at stake.

Before you get up to begin, pray for the ending. Claim God's help in getting the response He wants. Surrender your plans to Him, so that He is in control of events. There's no need for preachers to manipulate a crowd when the Lord turns up!

2. Use music well

Make sure your musicians know how to be sensitive to the moment. They should not distract from what the Lord is doing in people's lives, either by playing too loudly, or by changing their songs too often. If you're not sure that they can handle it, don't use them at this time. God doesn't actually depend on music backing!

3. Make clear what you want people to do

Tell people exactly what it is you are inviting them to do. Don't make wide sweeping statements like: 'I want you to step forward if you've ever had a problem . . . ' Be specific: 'I'd like to pray for you if right now you're suffering the pain of rejection.' Also, spell out what sort of response you're after: 'I'd like to ask you just to step into the aisle and come and join me at the front so that I can pray for you.' Public response of this kind can break all kinds of fear and pride barriers which might otherwise cause people to leave still carrying their pain.

4. Don't lie

Don't have people respond under false pretences. Don't say, 'I only want to pray for you' and then proceed to ask them all manner of personal questions. Don't tell them they're only coming for prayer if you plan to ask them into a side room afterwards. Be honest. It shows respect.

5. Be welcoming

Many preachers say 'Come' with their mouths, while their body language is nervously saying 'Stay back!' Make sure you relax people with your style. Don't come on like a high-powered insurance salesman; respect the individual's right to choose and admire the honesty of those who respond.

One of the reasons not much seems to happen at some response times is that people are too intense. We need to make them feel at home in God's presence, to give the Lord 'room to move'. When people lock up emotionally, even He finds it difficult to get right through to them and make a lasting impact. Of course I'm not advocating levity—I'm simply suggesting that it might be more effective to smile and shake someone's hand as they come, than to scowl and bellow at them in mock spiritual superiority.

6. Keep the audience involved

Don't allow people to drift off mentally while you're praying with or speaking to those who've come for help. Don't hand proceedings over to someone else unless you're actually finished (or unless the pastor wants you to), because people need to maintain a level of anticipation and hope as they come to pray. People respond best to you, the preacher, so keep your hand on things, building faith levels in hungry hearts and gently leading people to Christ.

7. Have your people-helpers ready

Some churches call them 'counsellors', but I prefer the word 'listener' because that's what every altar worker should be first.

Never take for granted that either your workers or

those who come forward for prayer actually know what they're doing! Workers need to be trained. People who respond to Christ for the first time need to have their need explained to them.

Billy Graham offers these insights:

> While we are taking for granted that all is well with new converts, cults assume that their new members know nothing. They start from scratch and build into the newcomer all the skill he or she needs . . . By assuming too much, we leave our new believers open and vulnerable to cults with their . . . pat answers.[2]

8. Know when to stop

It's so easy to get carried away on the euphoria of a moment of blessing. Don't ever let a meeting go from excitement to boredom simply because you've held on too long. It's always better to have people go away wanting more than to have them say: 'Doesn't that guy think we have homes to go to?' Be sensitive both to the Holy Spirit and to the people He is wanting to help.

Grandmothers used to say, 'A thing worth doing is worth doing well.' Rubbish! A thing worth doing is worth messing up a few times before you do it well. Even if you don't have the ability of Billy Graham, the confidence of Reinhard Bonnke or the experience of Paul Yonggi Cho, keep at it. If you're a preacher, be the best you can be—for heaven's sake!

2. Billy Graham, op. cit. p. 103.

6

Space Invaders

*He was the most other-motivated person in history.
In His mind, His own needs were placed behind
those of others. He followed this line of thinking
even to the point of cruel death. Today, churches
which do not live as He did—to reach out to
others—do not live for long! Outreach is the
lifeblood of the church. When we stop reaching out
we start fighting among ourselves: over what
'forms' of evangelism God can and can't use!*

Some things Jesus said were not very polite, were they? I
mean, He sometimes doesn't give you any room to
manoeuvre at all, does He? He says things like 'Go and
preach to every nation' (Mark 16:15, paraphrased), and, 'If
you're not really passionate about serving me, you make
me sick' (Rev. 3:16, paraphrased). Strong words!

Jesus spoke straight about outreach because He knew
the size of the need. He also knew just how frail we can be
sometimes—we need strong words to get us moving, to
break us out of our comfort zones.

Every Christian is built to be a space invader. We are
called to take our message to those who haven't heard, to
make Jesus King where He is not yet known. What makes
an outreach event a success, though? What can a leader do

to ensure maximum results? You must start by asking a straight question.

What Do You Want and Why?

Outreach events must always begin with the setting of goals. I don't mean simply numerical goals—though they're important—but basic descriptions of what you want to achieve in the community.

There's absolutely no point just running an event for the sake of it, or because the leader down the road has done it. You've got to know that this is a priority for you and why. You must know that it will meet a real need.

Too many church groups have a 'scatter gun' approach to outreach—they fire all their shot at nothing in particular. They 'aim' into the air, close their eyes and hope to hit something! It's time we started to focus a little more, to target specific objectives. As local churches we must ask two questions: what are the greatest needs in our communities? and what needs are we best qualified to meet? (What group should we be 'aiming at'?)

If you can't state in one sentence what you want your outreach to accomplish, you haven't thought it through clearly enough. I've been a guest at some events which have not been aimed at any real target. You feel as if you're power-walking through jelly—you use a lot of energy and get nowhere fast. If someone invites me to speak at an event, I like to be able to ask up front what its purpose is, so that I can submit to that vision. If the key leadership don't know where the thing's headed, everyone who's involved will stamp their own dream on it and it will take off in fifteen different directions at once.

Many leaders are afraid to talk about setting goals for events, especially ones which can be quantified and measured. They say God's not interested in numbers. What they really mean is: 'I'm afraid to set measurable goals.' After all, once we start talking figures, we've set ourselves up for scrutiny. People will be able to tell whether we reached the goal or not.

God *is* interested in numbers, because they are abstractions for people. He doesn't use numbers as His only measure of success, but numbers do matter to Him. (He even named a book of His Bible after them!)

Goal setting doesn't need to be so frightening. Consider the following lessons (learned the hard way!):

Goals are your servant, not your master

Some leaders allow their goals to rule their lives. They set goals which are unrealistic and, when practice can't match theory, they call themselves all the names under the sun. Goals are only facilitators—they give us something tangible to reach for and work towards. If we don't reach our goals on the first attempt, that's no reason to give up in disgust. If a goal's a good one, it's worth going for until we get it right.

Goals should be undercooked and overeaten

Sometimes in our enthusiasm to do our best for the Lord we set goals which neither we nor the people we lead can ever hope to achieve. A man came to me once and proudly announced that he had rented out the second largest sports stadium in our city. It would seat around 80,000 people and, though he had no organisation behind him and no real credibility with the churches, he planned a city-wide Christian praise meeting.

The whole thing was going to cost a fortune, but money's not a problem if you have God's vision and not just a good idea. Unfortunately this guy's meeting was just a good idea. After massive publicity and costly promotion the whole thing attracted just a thousand or so people—a very small proportion of the 80,000 seats.

His vision might have proved the right one in time. If he'd started off a little smaller it might eventually have come together on the big scale, when church leaders began to trust the vision. His goal was simply too large.

In situations like this one the goal sounds good when the event is still a long way off, but the closer we get, the more impossible it seems.

Business managers know that people are demotivated by failure. If they are revved up to achieve a certain level of success and they fall short, it can sap their energy for the future. So people in business will underproject and over-perform. That is, they set goals which are not too far out of reach and then go ahead and blow them away.

Let's say you want to run an event to reach 500 people. You don't tell your youth group that you want 500 people—you publicly set the number at more like 400. Then you work towards 500, so that when more than 400 people arrive, everyone feels good because they've cracked their goal!

The same approach is needed financially. You should plan to get less income than you actually hope for and your budget should be conservative. That way, when more than you need comes in, you have a faith-building bonus!

There are times when this approach isn't the right one—when the Lord speaks specifically to you about a certain goal. This is a word of faith and the Lord gives you the supernatural ability to believe for it. In normal circumstances though, the strategy described above is a good one.

Nail your colours to the mast

Some people like to set numerical goals and then hide them away. That's the easy way out. You must take the faith risk of declaring where you're headed and how much you think can be achieved. The book of Habakkuk tells us to 'write down the vision' (Hab. 2:2). It's only when we declare it openly that we can be held accountable for it. That alone will motivate us to achieve.

Goals alone won't make it happen

You can write down your goals until you develop arthritis, but they won't change a thing until you act upon them. Don't be like some leaders I've met who can always tell everyone else how to have success, but just can't quite crack it for themselves. They can even write books about how to reach the world, but they've never built a strong local ministry.

Who was it who said: 'Faith without works is dead'? (Jas. 2:26 KJV) That guy knew something.

Who Do You Want and Why?

OK, some goals have been set. You can say what you want to achieve and can measure whether you're effective. Now it's time to talk personnel.

Who is going to speak at this outreach? Or who is going to play? Who's going to be on the leadership team and who will work behind the scenes?

Here are a few tips to get you started on the right track:

Avoid ego-trippers like the plague!

Have you ever really admired someone until you got to know them?

Sadly, I've had experiences where I've worked with music groups and speakers whom people really admire from a distance, but who prove to be a real disappointment when you meet them up close. You know, they run around barking orders at everyone, or they send you a list of the three hundred things they require before they'll even come. They are superstars, when what you need are servants.

Forget those turkeys—no matter how talented or famous they may be. You don't need them, believe me. Go for people who want to see lives changed and the Kingdom, not their fan club, extended.

No outreach event should simply be a talent quest for people in your own group. People you promote must be gifted and anointed in their field. But you still have a choice to make: good performance alone or life-changing ministry. Go for the changed lives every time.

Avoid manipulators

A good vision can easily be hijacked by people who want to take your hard work and turn it to their own personal advantage. They like your dream but insist on making some 'minor' alterations if you want their support. Unfortunately, one man's 'minor' is another man's 'catastrophic'.

Don't think you have to please the whole of the church worldwide before you can get anything done for

God. I've sat in on some committees whose only motive for being seems to be the avoidance of conflict between their members. People are supposedly planning an event together, but all they're doing is trying not to offend each other. That's not unity, that's uniformity.

If God gives you a vision for an event, gather people around you who will make constructive changes, but won't try to sidetrack the whole thing according to their own agendas.

Look for loyalty as well as gift

Years ago I learned something which has stood me in good stead in running large public youth rallies. I was pastoring a youth group of 130 people and one year we ran a concert event which attracted over 800 people. We filled the local Town Hall and had over twenty people come to Christ.

The whole event was based on teamwork. The publicity materials were put together by gifted kids in the group. The ushering and security were handled by other kids. Another group put the refreshments together and still another worked behind the scenes on stage management and so on. We called in experts in sound and lighting but kept to our own people as much as possible.

Not only was the concert a great success as an outreach, but it did more to motivate our youth group than any amount of my teaching could have done. They had tasted success for God! Once you've tasted that, you're spoiled for anything less in life.

Years later I am still learning about building teams out of committed people. In our large Youth Alive rallies which attract thousands to major venues, we are seeing hundreds of people joining our volunteer work teams because they like the vision and the results.

These people are not all experts. Most are just enthusiasts. They are loyal to God's dream and will serve wherever they are asked. Obviously we try to fit people in wherever they are most likely to be effective according to their gifts, but while experts sometimes run around making demands, servants are preoccupied meeting the needs. Interestingly, servants sometimes do develop into experts, simply because their openness makes it easy for them to learn.

Make clear what you want people to do

People are motivated to achieve when they know exactly what it is that's expected of them. You need to plan as carefully as possible for every area of responsibility. Your security people must know what it is you want them to do, in practical terms—what time they're needed, what areas in the venue each one will cover, what they should do with any disturbance in the crowd and so on.

Your counsellors must know where they can talk to people, how they should present the gospel, what questions they should ask to ensure people know what salvation is all about. Your sound crew should know what time sound checks are on, what the programme is like in detail, what time dinner is and when the pre-outreach prayer meeting will take place. Every group should be involved like this weeks before the event, so that they are made to feel part of a team.

Delegate or die

If you are where the buck stops with an outreach event, there's no way known you can cover every leadership base yourself.

You might well be able to do a job better than one of your less experienced protégés, but that won't develop any new ministries, nor will it equip anyone for ministry. Remember: in the ministry of Jesus Christ we're not just interested in getting the job done, but in equipping and releasing other people to their potential. Besides, if you don't share the load you may run one great event, but it may only be one!

As the overseeing leader you will need to act more like a combination of visionary and manager. Your task will be to motivate other key people and to require that they answer to you and give you regular feedback.

You will need to spell out what each key person will be responsible for. Give them a job description—write it down if it helps—then trust them to do the job. Don't breath down their necks—make them aware of your confidence in them. Give them the authority their role requires and don't second-guess their decisions.

At the same time, ask for the feedback you need when you need it and always pass on information which might be helpful to your team. Never talk about your team in a disparaging way. If you have a problem with a team member, talk it through with the person face to face. Show a high level of loyalty to your team and expect it in return.

Look After Your Guests

Guest ministries should be treated with respect. Even servants need to be fed and given some time and space on their own. I've been the inviter and the invitee many times, so I've seen both sides. Let me suggest some items to mark in your list of things to do.

1. Finance

Make sure you have a budget for your speaker(s) or guest musician(s). So often their needs are only considered as an afterthought to be dealt with if there's a healthy profit at the event. It's a scriptural principle that workers deserve their wages (Matt. 10:10). You may like to ask your guests when you first invite them what they might need financially to take part in your event. This is especially vital when they have full-time itinerant ministries and no base of support aside from love offerings and the like. Please be sure that you don't promise what you can't deliver. It's better to underproject and overperform.

Also, if they have families to support you should consider giving more than you might if they were single. No employer expects people to work without financial incentive. Worthy ministers of the gospel are not in the work for the money, but they still need to pay the bills and to be free to attend to the Word and prayer (Acts 6:4).

Make adequate allowance too for larger groups. A music group cannot survive on the same honorarium as a solo singer.

2. Accommodation and travel

Ensure that your guests have privacy. Hotels are nice if you can afford them, but if the budget won't stretch to that find homes where people at least have a quiet and uncramped room. Try not to place guests with hosts who have large families—it can get difficult to use the bathroom. Basically it's in your interests to give a guest time to think, pray and relax.

Ensure that they can use the phone too (within reason of course). Try to tell them where they'll be staying before they arrive so that they don't come with any misunderstandings.

Visitors should not be expected to find their own meals, unless they wish to do that. Ask your guests when they would like to eat and try to work with their time-frame.

Remember, if your guests are worth inviting, the chances are they live by a very busy schedule and will go from your event to another next week. So look after their health and wellbeing.

Check with your guests as to whether they want you to make the travel arrangements, or whether they will do it and send you the bill. Make certain you have the travel details so that you know when they'll arrive and can meet them personally. If there is no booking of airline flights involved you should still commit yourself to cover fuel bills and the like.

Try to appoint a responsible and amiable leader (who owns a reliable car) to take responsibility for the needs of the guest while they're with you. If there are any important things you've overlooked, that person can attend to the need at the time.

3. Programme

Finally, make sure your guests know exactly what you want from them. Don't go over the top on this—some people almost tell you exactly what to preach!—but it is important to let them know what the programme looks like and what amount of time they have at the event. Please don't put speakers into the programme as an afterthought. Build the music programme around the speaker's role. Music alone is not usually enough to lead people to a sincere commitment to Christ, so make sure the speaker has a prominent position in the programme and is not cramped by band change-overs and the like.

It's not luxury that counts here—just consideration. If you treat your guests with respect you will be sowing good seeds for the future of your outreach programme. God blesses the generous of heart.

Promote! Promote! Promote!

It was a warm spring afternoon. I sat in the office of one of Australia's leading advertising executives. As a committed Christian he had managed to maintain a Christian ethic in what is one of the most competitive business arenas in our society. I was curious: how can the church get its message across to the masses? How can we compete with the huge mega-industries which saturate the airwaves with their message *ad nauseam*?

Our conversation was drawing to a close when he summed up the answer to my question very succinctly.

'There's one thing you must always remember, Mal,' he concluded. 'The church has the best form of advertising already going for it. The church has a huge network of word-of-mouth advertisers, the people who've had a real experience with Christ. Companies would kill to get hold of an advertising resource like that—they know that satisfied people are the best advertisement for anything.'

When it comes to promoting outreach events, our best strategy will be to get our own people so excited about it that they will take the initiative in spreading the word.

As a leader you can train your young people in things like giving an invitation. Many kids simply do not know how to get a message across to their friends. You can sow the seeds of creativity in their minds. For example, you can suggest practical ways in which students might spread the word on their school or college campuses: via the campus newspaper, through street theatre, with banners and posters and so on.

You can help them along the way by producing quality promotional materials. What does it take to put together good materials?

You don't need a million bucks!

Let's face it—you're not Coca-Cola. But you can put together quality posters, tickets and so on without mortgaging your house. If you have a talented artist in your group you're off to a great start, but make sure he or she has had some experience in working with printers and so on, or you may spend more than if you'd hired a professional.

Quality and value for money are the keys here. If necessary shop around until you find the best price. Always insist on seeing examples of an artist's or printer's work before you proceed. The cheapest is not always the best.

Remember: you are competing with a lot of other messages out there. You won't see a Rolling Stones album cover which has been run off on a photocopier. Aim for excellence and an attention-grabbing result.

Choose a theme or title which says it all

Your poster art should feature a title which sums up what the event's all about, but which definitely does *not* include Christian clichés!

It's a standing joke among some of my friends that I hate being billed as a 'dynamic evangelist' or 'anointed youth speaker'. Those terms and others like them have no

145

meaning at all to people outside the church (and very little meaning to people within the church!) Who uses words like dynamic—except in referring to politicians—and what in the world is an evangelist? OK, most Christians know what evangelists do, but you're not wanting to attract just the Christians to an outreach event. Try to find more up-to-date descriptions if you must use them at all. Be creative, don't be lazy.

Make your theme punchy but not offensive. I used to think the themes we use for Youth Alive rallies in Australia were aggressive until I saw some of the ones William Booth used in the early days of the Salvation Army. *They* got your attention!

The key is to present something which does not look like a church poster. If your advertising fits into what the public expects from the church, you'll always fail to grab their attention and hold their interest.

I must balance this by saying that you need to be honest about the event. Don't tell lies, such as 'Admission Free' when you will be taking an offering and asking for donations. It is possible to tell the truth without being negative—for example: 'No Door Price . . . Suggested Donation: £3.00'.

Don't be dishonest about who is providing the concert either, but try to find a creative name for your youth group. Lines like 'Brought to you by the First Church of the Real Truth Family Centre Incorporated' might read well on the church digest, but they don't do much for the MTV fan you're wanting to reach.

Tickets are not demonic!

Some people will complain that charging people for a Christian concert or other event is the same as charging people to hear the gospel. Or that doing so is a sign of the organisers' lack of faith. Sometimes, however, a minimal ticket charge for an outreach event is a good idea—for two reasons:

First of all, as these things get larger income from offerings and donations does not always grow in proportion to the growth in expenditure. Higher costs for larger venues can make it difficult to keep up.

Secondly, young people often have a greater sense of anticipation when some kind of door price is requested. That's because any other worthwhile event for youth incurs a ticket price. That price is a kind of guarantee that they'll get their money's worth, that they'll come away impressed with what they saw. So tickets have, in a sense, become part of the cultural language of the modern youth scene.

Of course, charging people to go to church is a different matter. Youth outreach events are designed to meet kids on their own turf, to introduce them to the claims of Christ in a culturally relevant—but biblically sound—way.

I find that when I go into a school and tell the kids I have some free tickets to give away to them, they respond more readily than if I say the event is free. Tickets are a symbol of value. Also, if you are forced to take more than one offering in an event, this is a worse witness than charging for tickets, as it makes God look miserly and His people unable to cover their bills.

Besides, I think Christian young people can learn to pay for their friends and youth leaders can hold fundraisers to pay for unsaved kids to attend an event. Of course, if costs are small, you might not need to charge a ticket price. That's probably a good place to start. You should not set out to make a huge profit as this tends to obscure the original motive—the salvation of souls—after a while.

But if you are spending wisely and economically and things are still falling behind, then it is worth considering. Just ensure that the price is minimal. Don't try to match it with secular ticket prices.

Making the media aware

If you're going to reach beyond the Christian culture, you may need to make use of the secular media to promote your event.

Don't be afraid to make contacts with key people in local newspapers and radio stations. Send them a one-page press release, which describes in punchy terms what the event is about, along with posters and any promotional materials you have on your guest speakers and performers. Perhaps send them some background on the history of the event. Ask them to advertise the event in community service announcements or to write an editorial about it. They might even like to interview the guests before the event so that an article has a personal, human-interest touch to it.

A press release must always include the time, place and cost of the event. Try to put things in as simple terms as possible. Don't clutter the information up with too many words. Try to include a photo of someone if you can. It is always more effective to send the release to a particular person rather than just to a post office box number. With newspapers try to send things to a prominent reporter; with radio or TV, make contact with key producers.

Once the press release has been sent, a follow-up phone call is worthwhile. Personal contact is much more likely to ensure some action.

Of course, if media people don't respond, don't give up, try again next time.

Just a little creativity and thoughtful planning can take you a long way in promoting an outreach. Remember though, the best advertising is by word of mouth: excited people inviting their friends.

Keep the Fruit

Jesus said that God is glorified when our fruit remains (John 15:16 KJV). Many times Christian events have given people a good time on the night, but the results for the Kingdom of God have been scarce and shortlived.

In order to keep the fruit you must set up a good follow-up programme. Someone must be appointed to oversee the training of counsellors and the collating of follow-up details. All counsellors should be given the same training and be giving out the same materials to their new friends—including a New Testament in plain English and a brief letter or tract outlining the plan of salvation. Counsellors should be 'prayed up' before the event so that they're sensitive to the Spirit as they talk to new converts.

It's a good idea to have a few specialist counsellors around too—people who can help kids who are having very specific problems with difficult issues such as incest or other forms of abuse.

If other church groups have supported your event, make sure you are fair in allocating new Christians to their nearest good church. The churches to which you refer them must preach the gospel and be committed to teaching the Word of God. If a young person has come with a friend, refer them to their friend's church wherever possible so that the relationship is maintained. Relationships, not bureaucracy, are the key to the growth of a new Christian.

It is a good idea to call these churches for a report a little after the event. This will help you to know whether the young person has been given adequate assistance in their new faith walk.

Pray Without Ceasing

Let's get one thing straight. Talent and careful planning are not enough to bring people to Christ. Only the genius of the Holy Spirit can do that (John 6:44). So don't be presumptuous enough to think you can get by without Him. Commit every step of the process to the Lord in constant prayer. He should be on the ground floor of every decision and each action. Every person on your leadership team should be a prayer warrior. If they're not when you start, they should be when you're finished with them!

'If the Lord doesn't build the house, the builders are working for nothing' (Ps. 127:1).

7

I Want to Plant a Church!

How did Jesus change the world? He did not set up a political party to make new laws. He did not leave us a Rotary Club to invest in new projects. His legacy was not an army to overthrow those who disagreed with Him. What agent of change did Jesus leave behind? He left only a church. A church that's been persecuted and sometimes very weak. A church that's been the persecutor and sometimes very wrong. But a true church which has never been wiped out. His church. The church He continues to build.

According to leading missiologists there are 24,000 distinct people groups in the world, half of which have never been effectively reached with the gospel. According to Jesus, the church's commission will not be complete until the gospel of His Kingdom has been preached 'to every nation' (Matt. 24:14).

The planting of new local churches is now recognised the world over as perhaps the most effective form of evangelism. It is one of the great keys to the growth of the Christian church throughout the world. Wherever the church is expanding rapidly today it is doing so because the ministries of ground-breaking apostles and evangelists are being complemented by those of pastors and church planters.

China had only one million Christians in 1949, yet today some estimates cite a Chinese Christian population of as many as 80 million. Most of this growth has occurred away from government-approved—and controlled—church denominations. It's happened in smaller local communities of believers who meet regularly—and often in secret—for worship, teaching and fellowship. Wherever the Spirit is moving in power, new churches are being born.

Other major church growth areas such as Brazil, Argentina, South Korea and parts of Africa have also seen a rapid increase in the rate of church planting. Mass evangelism via crusades and the like has been of little effect without fervent church planting. In fact, the greatest problem for the church in many of these growth areas is the lack of teachers to train the new pastors.

In more westernised countries, however, involvement in the local church is all too often low on the list of priorities for the individual Christian. Church planting is given very little prominence in the strategies of established denominations.

In his book *The Source*, James A. Michener cleverly uses an archaeological dig to track the development of Christianity alongside that of Judaism and Islam. At one point Eliav, the Jewish assistant archaeologist, is debating with John Cullinane, his Irish Catholic boss, the strengths and weaknesses of their respective religions.

'You Christians have beauty, passionate intercourse with God, magnificent buildings and frenzied worship . . . ,' says Eliav. 'But you will never have that close organisation of society, family life and the little community that is possible under Judaism . . . [Christianity] is totally incapable of teaching men to live together.'[1]

Sadly, that's the way many people in the West view the church of Christ—disjointed, uncaring and preoccupied with individualism. Yet Jesus told us that our love for each other would be the one great 'badge' of our discipleship (John 13:35). He said the world had the right to judge whether we served a real God by the quality of our relationships with each other. Jesus meant us to live in community, in harmony with other believers. We're none of us called to play Lone Ranger.

Jesus saw His church as the expression of God's love and power to the world. I've heard young people come out with things like this: 'I don't need to be part of a *local* church, because I'm part of the *universal, spiritual* church.' What a cop-out that is—and a cover-up for an unsubmissive spirit! Jesus didn't intend the church to be just some ethereal philosophical idea. He wanted real people in every community to be able to point to a real, tangible body of disciples and say: '*That's* what Jesus is like. *That's* what it means to follow Him.' Jesus wanted the local church to be an incarnation of Himself. The local church is God's 'shop window' to the world!

It is also the Lord's means of protecting, guiding and encouraging His people. He has placed resources within each church, via the different gifts in its people, to help Christians grow (Eph. 4:15–16). He has anointed leaders who are there to serve us and help us develop in our own callings (Eph. 4:11–12). You've got to have air between your ears if you don't want to enjoy everything

1. James A. Michener, *The Source* (Corgi Books, 1965), p. 780.

God has laid out for your own growth.

Oh, I know that local churches have flaws and they don't always do God justice. But, if you're willing to make allowance for the fact that churches are made up of flawed human beings, you may just find in them that sense of security and belonging Jesus intended for you.

We in the West need to wake up to our need of the local church. We should stop looking for the perfect church and contribute to the one we're in. (Someone said, 'If you find the perfect church, don't join it—you'll only spoil it!') And we must wake up to the challenge of church planting before we surrender a generation to Satan without a fight.

Young People Make Great Church Planters!

It's taken the church quite a few years to tap into the tremendous resource within its young people, especially in church planting. Some pastors have bemoaned the fact that they can't be adventurous in their outreach because they just don't have the 'right kind of people' to do it. Many times the right people are the people at hand—especially the young.

There are two reasons why church planting and young people make a powerful combination. First of all, young people *need* church planting. It provides great opportunities for them to develop their gifts and pursue heroic, risky Christianity. Many established churches lose their youth simply because they don't trust them with any great task.

I made my first overseas mission trip when I was 27

years of age. I visited Sri Lanka and Malaysia and it changed my view of world missions. That same year, with the support of my home church, I planted a new church in our city. I discovered that church planters are missionaries too. I think young people can learn a great deal about missions, about real on-the-edge faith living, *before* they ever head overseas—through getting involved in a church-planting scheme.

There's no greater school than the school of experience. My early experience in starting a new church and my subsequent oversight of other church planting work taught me a great deal about Christian life which I could not have learned in any other way. If you're young and you want to find out what real discipleship is about, get involved in a church-planting venture somewhere.

Church planting *needs* young people too. They bring to the task certain unique and vital qualities, one of which is *enthusiasm*. Excitement is absolutely essential in the launching of any new project or idea—and joining a church is a new idea for a great many people in society. When there's a healthy dose of enthusiasm around a new church, outsiders get interested.

In fact, many a great church started as a youth programme or children's outreach. Planting a church might seem out of reach for some reading this, but your faith might stretch far enough to start a new youth programme or home group in a neighbouring town. Go for it!

Boldness is a 'young quality' vital to church planting. Pioneers are people with an inbuilt sense of daring, a desire to push the limits. Getting involved in church planting is one way of tapping the prophetic rebel within young hearts! Because young people are attracted by shows of courage, a bold witness also attracts other youth in the community.

A third characteristic of the young is that they *'travel light'*. Young people on the whole haven't yet become entangled with mortgages or careers and family worries. They're able to 'hang loose', to throw themselves into new projects and give their all.

The fourth quality needed in any church-planting venture is *prayerfulness*. I would not want to suggest that young people have cornered the market on this one, but I've already said that young people will commit themselves to prayer when they're taught how heroic it really is.

Many of the greatest revivalists in history have been converted and pledged their lives to God's service while still in their youth. William Booth, founder of the Salvation Army, was just 15 years of age when he pledged himself to God's work. His wife Catherine did so when she was 17. William Carey, called by some 'the father of modern missions', was 18 when he made a commitment, as was D. L. Moody. Charles Spurgeon and Hudson Taylor were both 15, C. T. Studd and George Whitefield 16 years of age when their lives were committed to missions. Dr Billy Graham was just 17 when he devoted his life to the ministry of God's word.

Take a look anywhere in the world where there's a lot of church planting going on and you'll quickly discover that there are young people involved in the work.

What You Need to Pioneer a Church . . .

OK, let's assume that you're sold on the importance of evangelism and pioneering new churches. Let's also assume that you are in a church which has a vision and strategy for church planting. Oh, by the way, there's absolutely no reason why youth pastors can't initiate a church-planting vision in their churches. Sometimes, because youth leaders have all the youth resources at their disposal, they are the ideal people to facilitate local missions with the approval of their pastors. If your pastor doesn't seem too interested, it might be because he's not aware that anyone cares enough to get involved and take initiative.

For those who are serious about church planting, let's look at what it takes in more detail. Please note: these principles apply equally well to the starting of a new youth programme or home cell group. If that's where you're at, simply substitute 'youth programme' or 'home group' wherever you read 'church'.

First of all it must be said that there's no explaining why some churches grow more quickly than others. You simply can't make a science out of the sovereignty of God. You can't take out the textbooks, do everything the experts tell you to do, and expect to grow a church to make Dr Cho's look like a house meeting! You may be working in one area for months with little response.

However, there are some general principles which seem to apply in all churches which grow. There are some needs common to all church planting. I'd like to mention eight important ones:

1. A good relationship with a base church
For too long church planters have been expected to work 'solo'. Men and women have been 'released' to go out and break new ground without any support network or resource base. Instead of launching new people into ministry, we've made them walk the plank! When those same people fail,

lose their vision or simply wear out, no one accepts responsibility for their restoration or for the ongoing work of the fledgling pioneer church.

Larger churches have a responsibility to help establish new works. A new church needs financial backing, for the hire of meeting venues and, in time perhaps, for some level of wage for the pastor. It also needs creative and ministry support—especially in preaching and music. Perhaps most importantly, its leadership need to feel that they are part of something larger and more secure than just their own fellowship. They need to be able to network with other leaders, and to relate to fathers in the faith.

Church planters also have a responsibility—to be accountable to someone, both in general vision and with finances. People in a new church feel secure when they know that even their leader answers to someone and has some support.

Youth leader, why not get your group to take on full or part responsibility for the short- and medium-term support of a new church, providing resources for outreach and discipling? It is possible to plant new churches without this back-up, but it can be heart-breaking work, real burn-out material. We've lost too many good leaders this way.

Some pastors have never been involved in pioneering a church. It isn't everyone's calling after all. This should not prevent them from opening their hearts (and cheque books, if necessary) to fledgling works or leaders with initiative. We're not all called to foreign missions either, but that doesn't prevent our being practically supportive.

2. A clear target
Often churches are planted without any real thought as to

who they might reach. Not all communities are faced with the same pressing needs. In some areas, loneliness among the elderly or single parents is a major concern, in others unemployment, family breakdown or youth homelessness might be the greatest challenges. Not all local communities will be made up of the same groups of people either. Predominant age, interest and cultural groupings will vary from place to place.

No church planter should go to work without defining what the 'target' area looks like. He or she simply can't afford to risk the credibility and effectiveness of the new work by making unsubstantiated assumptions. The key word here is 'focus'. Without it anything we build is prone to be very shaky (Jas. 1:8).

In the long term, any church will gradually expand its areas of influence. But at the beginning, it's a good idea to do what you're best at. I once asked Reinhard Bonnke why his ministry had been so blessed. He was quick to give praise to God and added simply, 'I'm just a single-minded man.' He knows what needs he and his team are able and called to meet and he just gets on with the job.

There are some questions which should be answered long before the public meetings and outreaches commence—questions like: what are the geographic and social boundaries of my target area? What do people in this area think are the most pressing problems they face? What do they think of religion generally and the Christian church in particular?

There are a few ways of gathering information like this. One of the most effective is the door-to-door or street survey. A survey should begin with a pleasant introduction, telling the interviewee who is asking the questions on behalf of what church. Five to ten questions is enough and the first few should seek information about the community generally. Towards the end there might be a question like this: 'As a new church in town we are anxious to be of real service to the community. If there were one need you think we could help meet, what would it be?'

You have gained valuable information on your area and at the same time announced that a caring church is coming to town.

One fledgling church in the USA researched its local area surveying hundreds of people about why they did not attend church. The answers were revealing. Some said, 'The church is always asking for money.' Others answered, 'I can't relate to the ministry or the music.' Still others offered these answers: 'The services are too predictable and boring' and 'The church makes me feel guilty.'

Today that church numbers in excess of 18,000 people. They tried to shape their programmes to fit the concerns expressed in these surveys, presenting Christ through meeting real needs.

Another tried and proven way of identifying needs in the community is to conduct phone polls. Local phone books can be used to poll people on general questions of community need, but people need special training in doing this work. In all survey work, people must state whom they represent at the outset, so that the church is kept above reproach.

Sometimes surveys can be followed up with public meetings, organised by the church but without any church trappings. These are not preaching or worship sessions— they are opportunities for members of the community to discuss an issue which has come out of your survey work. They demonstrate that the church is 'in it for the people' and not for proselytising alone.

Local councils possess volumes filled with helpful information on demographics and interest groups in the target area. They are a rich source of information and a few days spent poring over their material can get you off to a good start.

3. *The pursuit of excellence*

In the Middle Ages, the church led the way in the arts. If someone wanted to show off a work of art, they did it in a cathedral. Bach would sign some of his music, 'To the glory of God'. Michelangelo would study the Bible to find how to sculpt just the right image of David. In the 1990s a work of popular art is shown in a cinema while we in the church often find ourselves 10 years behind the culture. What is commonplace in the world today won't be accepted in the church for another decade, even if it is morally acceptable to us. We've given up our leadership in the arts.

Some people in modern churches have what I call a 'contemporary-phobia'. Anything in church life invented after 1790 is to be avoided at all costs— and music with a rock beat is played backwards to unveil secret Satanic messages!

Study church history and you'll see that every major spiritual revival has involved new forms of expression. Church pioneers have set the trends rather than followed them. Music provides a good example. Song writers like Luther, the Wesleys and Booth were all musical eclectics— they borrowed musical forms from the world around them, giving them religious themes. Luther took pub songs and made them into Christian classics. Today, it's not possible to reach a generation raised on rock, pop and heavy metal using forms which were in vogue 50 or 100 years ago.

161

New churches attract people when they speak the cultural language of the day *without* compromising the Bible. Original songs have proven to be a real bonus in many growing churches. They have a freshness which is aligned with the church's pioneer spirit and they help communicate to newcomers the self-image and style of the church.

We've already discussed the importance of excellence and creativity in preaching and teaching. The Word of God is powerful to affect every area of human life. One great message inspired by the Holy Spirit can often accomplish more than weeks of counselling or planning. As the church's members are equipped through teaching they will meet the needs of others around them. Sadly, some leaders spend all their time counselling or concocting intricate outreach programmes and allow their preaching skills to die.

We should be aiming for excellence in everything we do for God. Even the equipment we use and the buildings we rent say something about Him. It seems churches are prone to follow one of two extremes here. Either they fall for the so-called 'Prosperity Doctrine' (blab-it-then-grab-it!) or they follow the Franciscan path (God is glorified when you live in snivelling poverty). Neither is particularly biblical.

For one thing, Scripture says more about provision than prosperity. The very word 'provision' gives us a hint as to how God works. He provides *for the vision* He places on our hearts (pro-vision). When He has called us for something, He will equip us to carry it through (Heb. 13:20–21). He's not into extravagance but efficiency and accountability.

On the other hand, God hates poverty—on this the

entire record of Scripture is clear. Poverty demeans humanity and the Lord calls us to stand up practically for those who suffer in its grasp (Lev. 19:9). Poverty is *not* of itself glorifying to God. After all, human greed is not the sole property of the rich.

It is possible to walk the line between these extremes, to achieve excellence without extravagance. It *is* possible to combine excellence with anointing!

4. An appreciation of what went before

The major thing we learn from history is that we don't learn from history. Many churches are filled with contemporary-phobics. Just as many are ruled by contemporary-addicts. With these people anything invented before last Wednesday morning is anathema! They claim that all tradition must be swept aside for God to move.

However, it is impossible to last long as effective pioneers without an appreciation for the good people who have gone before us. Some church planters pull down the achievements of others who have gone before. They mistake tradition for traditionalism.

Traditionalism is the worship of tradition, or refusing to hear a new word from God unless it lines up with your tradition. In that sense the seven last words of a dying church are: 'It's never been done this way before.' A refusal to change is akin to Pharisaism, which closes in people's faces the door to God's Kingdom (Mark 7:6–9).

Tradition may sometimes be a poor master, but it is certainly a very good servant. There's a great deal of good to be said for tradition. The Bible is filled with good traditions—we call them doctrines. Without an understanding of sound doctrine as it has been passed down to us we are opening ourselves to error. There is protection in knowing how great past leaders wrestled with the questions of faith. There is great strength to be gained, too, from learning about the roots of our beliefs and our denominational movements.

We ignore the lessons of the past at our risk. Every church planter should learn as much as he or she can from past moves of the Spirit. Some young leaders are very gung ho about things. They rush into a new venture filled with all kinds of dreams about how they're going to do things the way they've always wanted to. Sadly, many learn the hard way that not all that's old is bad.

5. Creative promotion

The church has often fallen way behind secular culture in the use of print and electronic media. A new church needs to make people aware of its presence in town and what it has to offer. Some of us think that using the media is a high-cost strategy, that we can't afford it. Once again, a little creativity goes a long way.

Radio is perhaps the most underrated of all of the modern media available to the church. While TV advertising might be outside a pioneer church's price range, radio stations are often a cheaper and more effective alternative. They can be more fruitful because they allow a variety of programme formats—talkback, documentary, music formats and so on.

In many urban and rural areas there are regional community-based radio networks which rely on the work of volunteers in their service of local needs. Church leaders can become involved in presenting programmes on these stations, usually with very little financial outlay. If the new church can find a weekly sponsor and is prepared to abide by the rules of the station, it can easily lift its profile in town.

6. Good follow-up

Once people have started to attend meetings, or have expressed an interest in what the church is doing, they must be followed up by trained people who can explain further the vision of the church. Any materials which are given out should be well packaged.

People who attend the first meetings might be encouraged to fill out response cards which will show you if your programmes are meeting the needs. These can also allow people to request practical help (with child minding, etc.) or counselling.

Many leading companies require their executives to spend some time per month 'out in the field' dealing directly with customers and their problems. This sharpens their sense of what the customer wants from the company. Church leaders would do well to invest time in regular 'meet the people' exercises too. Even in pioneer churches, there's a real temptation for leaders to build impregnable walls around themselves. They insist that people can only ever see them by appointment. It would be refreshing to see pastors who make appointments to see their people!

7. The appreciation of team ministry

There's a lesson which some leaders learn the hard way: delegate or you die! Moses was anointed by God and then called by God to disseminate, to share that anointing (Num. 11:16–17). He simply couldn't do it all himself. The church leader must learn early on to facilitate the vision of other key people around him or her.

Churches which grow are churches which release people into their God-given potential. The pioneer pastor who is willing to appoint other gifted leaders to positions of influence sends a powerful message to his congregation. The message is this: in this church we'll stretch you and let you grow.

Most new churches need good leadership in areas such as youth ministry, children's work, creative ministries, follow-up and pastoral care. God will only bring the talent along if we're prepared to make use of it. If we don't release others, even the talent we do have in the church will be removed (Mark 4:25).

8. The appreciation of other expressions

There's nothing more off-putting to a newcomer to church than a leader who's constantly denigrating the work of other Christian groups. In my country, the fastest-growing church group are the Pentecostals. That wasn't always the case, however. In the 1970s a charismatic renewal swept through large sections of the established church groups in Australia, and the Pentecostals could only stand back and watch as these older groups—many of whom had long been antagonistic to the Pentecostal experience— flourished.

In some countries this kind of thing has caused deep resentment in the Pentecostal and evangelical scenes. (It's interesting to note how quickly we come to think we've cornered the market on truth.) To their credit though, the Australian Pentecostals did not dig in their heels and cry foul. They welcomed what God's Spirit was doing among their more traditional brothers and sisters. In the process they sent out a powerful message to the community and opened themselves to embrace a fresh move of God. Today they're experiencing ongoing growth.

When it comes to the Kingdom of God there's no

room for 'you in your small corner and I in mine' thinking. We need not be threatened by each other—there's plenty of blessing to go around. Besides, the more nets there are in our corner of the ocean, the more fish we'll catch.

If the church down the street is growing faster than ours, there's no reason why we shouldn't rejoice with them—and learn what we can from their success. If they're hurting, we should give them support (Rom. 12:15). It is true that leaders should protect their people from falsehood, but even that can be done in a way which does not put people down. There is such a thing as 'speaking the truth with love' (Eph. 4:15).

Getting Started . . .

Now you know what's needed. But how do you actually get something off the ground? Every church-planting exercise will be different from any other. There will be unique challenges and needs which will require creative thinking and prayer. However, I think we can safely say that there will be three groups of people involved at various stages of the pioneer programme:

Stage 1: Short-term blitzers
In Stage One there are three keys: outreach, outreach and outreach. This is the stage where any Christian leader can become involved in church planting—even those for whom pioneering is not their major call.

Your only aim here is to make the community aware that a new church is being started. You need to demonstrate a commitment to meeting real needs in a positive way, without denigrating any other churches in the area.

People of all ages can easily be enlisted for teams who will spend three or four weekends evangelising in schools, colleges, shopping centres, concerts, outreach meetings and on the streets. Teams might be ten to twenty people strong (when they get much larger than that they cause logistic nightmares).

Some team members might be Christians who are already living in the area and are eager to become part of the new work. Others can be drawn from the base church or organisation, or from several churches which share a common vision. There's absolutely no reason why Christians from different fellowships can't get involved in a new venture together, especially in an area where no one church is large enough to offer all the necessary resources.

Several pastors or youth leaders might be asked to release, say, five people for a definite period of three or four weekends. These selected recruits must commit themselves to keeping their pastors up to date with progress as the outreach unfolds.

Once the team has been selected the people need to be briefed on the aims and the strategies you'll be using. You'll need to get some workshops happening, to develop the skills you want to use. Some of your team may already be specialists in areas such as music or drama. Others will need to be trained to conduct surveys or to be involved in street evangelism. It's always best to assume people know too little rather than too much.

When the briefing is done, the teams can be released to 'blitz' the town. In physical warfare any attack requires careful pre-planning, and invading Satan's turf in spiritual warfare takes the same commitment to strategy. You should divide up your 'target' area into zones and designate different people or events to each area at different times. Drama, outdoor concerts, puppet shows for kids, free film screenings are all ideas which can be used to great effect.

If the mother church has a pastor in mind to take on the new work, it's a good idea to involve that person somewhere at this early stage. This helps them to become familiar with the local people, and vice versa. It also means that the prospective pastor has a chance to move elsewhere if he or she doesn't feel settled there.

When the initial period of outreach is finished, gather the team for a review of all that's been done. Look honestly at the impression you've made on the community and note the areas where you may need to improve your image. Feedback, they say, is the breakfast of champions. If that's true, then feedback is the breakfast, lunch and dinner of Christian pioneers. People need to know how they've done. Success breeds confidence for the future.

Some of the people in the team might be staying on to help with Stage Two. For the others, these wrap-up sessions are their opportunity to testify about what they've learned and to make new commitments to their own fellowships.

Stage 2: Medium-term bridgers

Let's assume now that you plan to stay on to Stage Two. Of course, even if you don't you can be involved in facilitating it.

This is the stage at which the church needs people with some experience in leadership. Any church is only as strong as its foundation. When you're working with a group of completely 'fresh' recruits, it can take two years or more to discover and develop true leadership abilities.

If some of your original team can remain behind, even for a while, or if you can recruit experienced Christians without robbing other churches to do so, your work will be made much easier.

The more key people you can draw from the local area the better, as this will help you build a truly local church.

In the establishment phase you are following up initial contacts and building lasting relationships with new people. You're constructing bridges with the people you've met.

The emphasis will change from outreach alone, to outreach combined with pastoring, counselling and corporate worship. The fledgling church will need teaching on the basics of Christian living—practical instruction on how being a Christian will influence daily life. You will need to instruct people in how the church is set up: what the ministry gifts are, how public worship works and how people can be released into their potential for God. You will need to preach a positive message of faith combined with straight talking about repentance and the cost of discipleship.

This is where it's important to ensure that financial accountability is in place. You may select a small group of your most trustworthy people to serve as a type of church council which administers finance. It's best to make any appointments only temporary ones at this stage, so that people see that leadership authority must be earned. This also gives you the opportunity to move people on if they prove unsuitable.

At this time you begin to set up long-term programmes for the growth of the church: home groups, children's church, Sunday school, youth groups and the like.

Stage 3: Long-term builders

You may feel the need to pull out of involvement after Stage Two. Perhaps as a young leader your level of experience has been fully exhausted at this point. There's no shame in admitting it—the important thing is what's best for the church. Churches should not be planted to boost our egos.

On the other hand, you may feel God's call, with the support of your oversight and the church members, to stay on to pastor the new work. This may mean a break from whatever other pastoral responsibilities you had previously. It might mean taking a risk. You certainly cannot pastor and grow a church without giving yourself to it wholeheartedly. The members of the new fellowship must be given the sense of dignity which comes from having their own pastor, not someone else's 'leftovers'.

Whether you go on to pastor the new work, or someone else steps in, the mother church must continue to offer what support it can until the work is really standing on its own.

The bottom line in all this is: every young leader who has the resources should become involved in planting a new church, youth group or even home group—if not in direct leadership, then in helping to provide the support and resources needed to pull it off.

8

Why the Devil Doesn't Have All the Good Music!

We don't know much about how Jesus sang. Perhaps the disciples had a really good choir happening. Maybe they featured Peter, James and John with a kind of Beach Boys harmony pattern. Who knows? Musicologists know very little about the way Hebrew music worked in the time of Jesus. He did sing, though (Matt. 26:30). He knew the power of music as a form of expression—both for contemplation and for celebration. He probably had a rich baritone voice too.

Good news! Even in the 1990s, the devil definitely does not have all the good music. Wherever spiritual revival is breaking out throughout the world today, new music is there lifting God's people into a fresh adoration of their Father.

I know there is also a lot of profiteering going on in the Christian music scene and we have a right to feel angry about it. Some parts of the so-called international Christian music 'industry' exist for the sole purpose of selling records to pay the wages of people who sell records, and so on *ad nauseam*. The industry has become, as the very word suggests, a self-propagating, self-serving machine which is more often about turning over product than it is about real ministry to people's needs. Somewhere in all that, the music gets buried under promotional hype.

The French Christian thinker Jacques Ellul could have had the Christian music industry—not the music itself—in mind when he said: '[Today] everything has become 'means'. There is no longer an 'end', we do not know where we are going . . . we set huge machines in motion in order to go nowhere.'[1]

Don't get me wrong here—there are some very good and godly people in Christian music circles. It's sad that they have to be part of what is such an ungodly system at times. It's sad to read some of the pre-tour material which goes out to concert promoters on behalf of Christian artists. I mean, how seriously can you take someone who is asking for a certain type of confectionery backstage before a 'show'? How interested in serving humanity are people who insist on flying everywhere first class and being chauffeur driven to each 'gig'? Where's the Christian distinctiveness in all this—what makes us any different from the money-crunchers in the pagan world?

I'm not saying we shouldn't protect and look after prominent Christian musicians. Life in the public eye can get pretty demanding, I suppose. I am saying that we should all grow up and look for super-servants instead of superstars!

---

1. Jaques Ellul, *The Presence of The Kingdom* (Helmers and Howard, 1989), p. 53.

The Power of Praise

Some of the most exciting advances in Christian music right now are being made not in the fields of entertainment or even evangelism—which are both valid and important but in local church worship and praise. It seems that many young leaders who are in the forefront of what God is doing know how to bring people together in corporate praise. What does it take to be an effective, even exciting, worship leader?

Before we answer that we should understand just *why* praise is important. Most of us go to church week in and week out; we sing the right songs and say all the right words, but we don't often ask one of the most important of all life's little questions: 'Why?' When we stop asking the 'why' question in any area of life, we stop striving for a better way and reaching for excellence. We sink back into mediocrity. We'd all be better equipped for praise and worship if we knew why we did it in the first place. So let's start there.

We praise God because He deserves it—and requires it!

God gets a kick out of our praise. God has put within everything He made a song of praise and celebration. The Old Testament is filled with lively references to trees that clap their hands and mountains that get down and boogie! (Isa. 55:12) All creation was originally designed to party and, while sin has spoiled the fun in many ways, you can still hear the music flowing through if you listen hard enough.

Man is the pinnacle of God's created order on

Spaceship Earth, so you'd expect he'd have the greatest capacity for praise. We were created for God's pleasure (Rev. 4:11; Col. 1:16). Show me a person who knows how to put God's pleasure first and I'll show you a person who gets a buzz out of living.

Modern man lives pretty much for himself. He considers the idea of pleasing anyone before himself some kind of restriction. He lives as if God were made in *his* image. Surrounded as we Christians are by this humanistic positivism, even we tend to do things because we enjoy them, or because they're healthy or beneficial for us. Ultimately though, we should do what we do because God wants it done.

The word 'worship' comes from two words in the old English: 'worth-ship', the assigning of value or worth to someone. Life only really takes off when we assign ultimate value to God our Creator. When Peter made his great confession, 'You are the Christ the Son of the living God' he was met with this response from Jesus: 'You are Peter, [the rock]' (Matt. 16:18). It's only when we recognise God in *His* proper place that we discover who *we* really are. A man devalues himself to the extent to which he values— and gives himself to—anything above God.

We praise God because we love His presence

The psalmist had a way with words. He said that God 'inhabits' the praises of His people (Ps. 22:3 KJV). The Hebrew word used there means 'to sit down', 'to settle into'. Think of yourself sinking into that favourite beanbag chair at home, or getting cosy in your water bed. That's how God responds to loving praise.

The Japanese have a great understanding of this. Traditionally, the emperor would be carried through the

176

streets as his adoring people bowed to him. I'm told that one Japanese translation of Psalm 22:3 has it this way: 'When God's people praise Him, they build Him a throne and He comes to sit in it.' Fantastic!

In the Old Testament, the ark of the covenant represented the presence of God with His people of Israel (Num. 7:89; Exod. 25:22). As the tangible symbol of God's presence the ark brought the Hebrews victory in battle (Josh. 6:6–21). It brought them guidance whenever God spoke from the mercy seat (Josh. 7:6–15). It brought prosperity—one guy called Obed-Edom made some great business deals while the ark rested in his home! (2 Sam. 6:11–12)

Today we do not have an actual, physical ark to look to, but the presence of the Holy Spirit still brings victory, guidance and blessing. Praise is a vehicle through which we come into a sense of God's nearness. The problem in many churches is not dry services but dry servants! We need to spend more time drinking in God's life-giving presence.

We praise because it is a powerful weapon in our armoury

When you read Judges 6, you begin to wonder why God went to so much trouble just to get Gideon to blow a trumpet. This guy was hiding in a winepress yet God set him aside to muster the men of Israel for war. Certainly he's an unlikely hero.

Somewhere underneath the layers of fear and defeatism in Gideon's heart, however, God saw a desire to fight back under the pressure. When Gideon eventually blew his horn he was calling the Israelites to recognise the strength of their God. He was declaring that, although they

177

were mightily outnumbered, they would come out the win-
ners because, and only because, God was with them.

Today many Christians are hiding in winepresses,
afraid to let their dreams right out lest they be squashed.
So many have lost their resolve to fight back when in a
corner. In these pressured times we need to sound the
trumpet of war again, declaring that God is on our side.

In a sense praise is the blowing of a trumpet which
declares that, whatever the enemy does, God and His
people will be victorious. Spiritual battles cannot be
fought with natural weapons (2 Cor. 10:3–4) and praise,
being a spiritual weapon, has the power to frustrate the
works of Satan (Ps. 149:6–9). Praise is a faith activity
because it gives thanks for the victory before it arrives.

Follow the Leader . . .

Corporate and personal praise is important for all kinds of
reasons. According to Jesus the important thing for us to
consider is not whether to spend time in praise, but how to
go about it. He taught that God is looking for people who
will worship Him the way He wants them to. He isn't so
concerned about the forms of music we use or the type of
liturgy our church is into; He's interested in our attitude of
heart (1 Sam. 16:7b).

People who can lead others in praise and worship
understand the attitudes God is looking for. Here are just a
few:

1. Holiness
I've read a lot about what it means to be holy. Let me offer
you my humble definition of holiness: holiness is living

out in my life what I know is true of God. Jesus said that we should worship in 'spirit and truth' (John 4:21–24). To be true means to line up my life with God's will, to serve with integrity, with nothing shameful to hide (1 Pet. 2:22). It means to be true to His nature.

Holiness is a decision. For example, because I know God doesn't lie (Num. 23:19), I will tell the truth. I understand that God is patient (Ps. 86:15), so I won't fly off the handle when someone offends me. God forgives (Ps. 103:3), so I won't harbour long-term grudges. If I seek to line up my behaviour and attitudes with those I see in the Lord, I can't help but lead a holy life.

Of course, the practice is never as easy as the theory. If it wasn't for the Spirit's daily infilling, we couldn't sustain it at all. Every one of us lives with a Barabbas inside us—the Bible calls him the 'old self' or the 'sinful self' (Eph. 4:22). Barabbas was a murderer and a thief and even the best of us are no better than he before we come to Christ. Just as the people in Jesus' day had to choose between Barabbas and the Lord (Matt. 27:15–22), so must we every day of our lives. We can release either in our dealings with God and man. In all that we do, we will release either the bully or the servant, the hater or the carer, the selfish one or the giving one. One or the other will rule our lives.

Holiness is releasing the Jesus within and crucifying Barabbas. Without holy hands and a clean heart I will never be effective in leading praise (Ps. 24:3–4).

2. Enthusiasm

Have you ever met a 'mega-spiro'? They're the ones who come to church carrying huge King James family Bibles. They're always quoting Scripture verses they don't

understand, just to demonstrate their superior brand of spir-
ituality. They claim to have real joy, 'deep joy'. The problem is their joy's so deep you can't find it! They look as if
they've been baptised in lemon juice.

I have a feeling God enjoys their company about as
much as I do. After all, God invented enthusiasm. In
Genesis, God was thrilled by what He'd made (Gen. 1:31).
There are many verses which talk about God being interested in and enthusiastic about His creation—especially
humankind. There's even one Scripture verse which says
that God wants to 'rejoice over' us, or, in the original language, to 'jump for joy, skip, leap and spin around' us
(Zeph. 3:17).

David knew how to lead praise. He whirled about so
much that his wife accused him of going too far (2 Sam.
6:20). Interestingly, he was wearing the linen ephod of a
priest when he did this, which shows us that enthusiasm is
not irreverent or distasteful to God. It's part of our priestly
ministry.

Of course, there are those who want to make an exhi-
bition of themselves just to get attention, but that's not
where David was coming from. He genuinely wanted to
express his joy to the Lord.

You just can't lead praise effectively unless you look
as if you're really enjoying it. People need a role model.
Ten years ago I was the youth pastor of a growing church.
We met in an old Town Hall. Every Sunday night it was
my job to walk onto the stage and create something out of
nothing. I had fifteen minutes to get the place hopping, so
that the pastor could jump in when the crowd were warmed
up.

It was a daunting thing—a bit like being thrown to

the lions, except that lions smile more as they eat you alive! These people would walk into church looking as if they'd gone ten rounds with Ali. You couldn't imagine a harder group to get excited about praise.

One night I discovered a little trick which got things going more than once thereafter. I developed a very close friendship with a particular brick in the back wall. As people dragged themselves into church, I'd smile at this brick in the distance. It's amazing how many people thought I was smiling at them and they returned the favour. Soon I started waving at the brick. Again, people thought it was aimed at them, so they responded. Before long I'd managed—through sneaky means, I'll confess—to convince a few of them actually to *enjoy* church. All it took was someone to set the tone of things.

Remember: wherever there's a David there's usually a Michal. Don't let them get to you—God loves enthusiasm.

3. Self-denial

I remember the first time I ever raised my hands to worship in church. I was a teenager, sitting with my friends at the back of the small wooden building. From that vantage point we used to chuckle at the hats the old ladies wore and generally heckle each other. This particular morning the Lord heckled me.

We were in the middle of a song when I felt a very strong impulse to raise my hands. Being the coward that I am I kept them firmly by my side. The still small voice inside said: 'I thought you said you loved me.' 'I do,' I replied mentally. 'Then why can't you express it?'

The impression was so strong that I eventually

lifted those hands to chest height, then slowly to head level, then all the way up, as if someone had put a gun in my back. That small act set me free from a binding sense of self-consciousness. I've never had a problem with my hands since. Self-denial is liberating.

David knew this. In his time, it was not uncommon for a court jester to walk before the king in any royal procession through the streets. His job was to make the people feel good about their monarch, so that by the time he'd finished with them they'd be singing the king's praises, even if they were being taxed to the hilt.

On the day David danced before the ark, he recognised that the real King of Israel was her God. For one day he stepped down from his throne and took the place of court jester. He laughed and the people laughed with him. He sang his latest psalms and the crowds joined in on the chorus. He led not just with enthusiasm but also with self-denial, and God loved him for it.

Self-consciousness takes on a number of faces. For some people it takes the form of egoism. In worship ministry we need big hearts, not big heads. That also applies to those who play the music—they are praise leaders too. If you have musicians who think they've just fallen out of heaven, pack them off marked 'return to sender'. Talented people have a responsibility to use their gift for service. When God gives you a lot, He expects a lot (Luke 12:48).

For other people, inferiority is the problem. One of Satan's favourite ploys is to accuse the worship leader of hypocrisy. 'You don't feel enthusiastic about God today and you know it!' he riles. 'You have no right to be up front when you feel so bad.' We must keep in mind the fact that praise involves faith as much as any other Christian discipline. We praise not by impulse, but out of obedience. Worship is not an act of whim, but of will. It is outside the realm of pure feeling, so we can shrug off the enemy's jibes.

A self-conscious attitude can also be expressed in unsubmissiveness. In the golden days of the Old Testament temple, during Solomon's reign, teachability was a key requirement for all the worship personnel. Leaders and musicians had to be open to correction and eager to learn (2 Chr. 23:8). I've seen people with attitude problems because they're musically more literate than their pastors. They think they can bypass the normal chain of command because they're creative people, and everyone knows how temperamental musicians are! (That's a massive cop-out: they're no more or less moody than anyone else.) All the really good musicians I've met have been soft and teachable. It's only less talented ones who think they have something to prove.

In the days of Solomon the temple musicians, who had been specially selected and trained for their posts, were also expected to carry out more mundane duties around the place (1 Chr. 9:22–32). Their membership of the worship team was not an excuse for avoiding other responsibilities. Humility is a key quality in good praise leaders.

So is a forgiving spirit. We should not bring our gripes and grumbles into the praise service (Matt. 5:23–24). Powerful, life-changing praise springs out of a spirit of unity and mutual respect (2 Chr. 5:13; Ps. 133).

How to Kill a Worship Service!

I've seen many leaders absolutely massacre what could have been great times of praise and worship—almost as if they were *trying* to wreck them. So I thought, why not put down some thoughts on how to make a *proper* hash of it? There are obviously a lot of leaders who'd take them on board. (Of course, if you're one of that rare breed who actually want to lead praise well, just reverse the principles.)

Don't pray . . .

It just may be that God has a certain plan for your worship time and, well, we can't have Him interfering in our set ways, can we? I mean, if we really were to hear from God, the praise might just lift into a new dimension.

Don't ever rehearse the songs . . .

Unfortunately, there's no way of avoiding success if you get along to regular rehearsals with the musicians. Before long you'll find yourself coming in on the right note and beat every time and never needing three runs through the introduction. The congregation will enjoy the songs more because they'll have learned them correctly the first time. You'll also know which songs can flow easily together, which means you won't have time to relate a favourite anecdote, or read Psalm 119, between each of them. Couldn't have that, could we?

Treat the musicians like dirt . . .

Ahhh, there's nothing like a good scowl or cynical jibe to turn the musicians or sound technicians right off you. Once you have them offside you can rely on a totally hard atmosphere. Just what you want.

Try to choose songs which have no connection with each other . . .

You'll be amazed at the difference it can make to your

worship service if you run songs together which have to-tally different tempos. This can really throw people into a spin. It's fun to watch.

Sing the same songs for thirty years . . .
People enjoy variety and the Holy Spirit often brings new life through fresh songs, so make sure you avoid contact with anything written in the last thirty years.

If you sing a meaningful old hymn, turn it into a dirge . . .
Let's face it, some saints of old did write songs which can get people excited even today. If you must use these songs, sing them at half speed, or hold on to notes in all the wrong places, or make sure the overhead projectionist doesn't have the words. Don't give the suckers an even break!

Sing each song once then preach a sermon . . .
You can't afford to let people get into the spirit of a song, especially if it has the potential to say something in and of itself. So cut the song off before people start enjoying it too much. Then you have lots of time to trot out your five favourite sermonettes.

Lead like a wet fish . . .
Under no circumstances must you provide strong leader-ship during the praise time. Let someone else set the tone—the musicians, the congregation, the cleaner, anyone but you. If brother so-and-so up the back wants to wait until a quiet spot in the service and then break out with his tired old favourite, let him do it. In fact, try to leave as many blank spots as you can to encourage

would-be Pavarottis to do their thing.

Try to sing as many different harmony parts as you can so that no one has any way of knowing what the melody sounds like. Also, fidget with your tie or microphone lead the whole time so that you don't look relaxed or in control. That would only inspire the people to feel confident.

Ignore microphone technique . . .

Nothing is less distracting than a leader who knows how to use a microphone well! Make sure you tap it, blow into it, or say 'Am I on?' at least ten times in the service. Don't be afraid to drop a microphone or two or to put one near the speakers so they whistle, if that helps.

Have people dance who don't know how . . .

Here's an old chestnut. Form a troupe of dancers in your church. Make the primary qualification for membership that they be greatly overweight or completely free of any gift in keeping time with music. Don't give them any training and don't require that they practise. Just give them a few coloured ribbons and let them go 'as the Spirit moves them'.

Drag the whole thing on until it dies a natural death . . .

If you're ever tempted to close the praise session on a 'high', resist, resist, resist. You must wait until the peak has been reached and then take the people on, down the other side. The preacher should never—repeat *never*—get to the pulpit feeling the people are hungry for what he has to say! He should have to work as hard as you have for response.

When there's a guest speaker or a big shot you want to impress in the service, add another fifteen minutes to your normal time-frame. Give them a good look at your style. Who cares if the meeting died in the first ten minutes?

Well, there it is: a comprehensive guide to ruining a worship session. If you follow these principles you can't go *right*. I wish you well . . . and hope we never meet in a church service!

9

Where Have All the Fathers Gone?

*This is not the place to be if you have a bad heart!
It's the Olympic Games in the year 2000. The crowd
is on its feet as the relay race is about to be run.
The air is so thick with excitement you can almost
reach out and touch it. People from almost every
nation on earth are packed into the enormous stadium in your city and the first runners have lined up
ready for the starter's gun.*

You're nervously warming up a few hundred metres down
the track, sweating with anticipation. You're number three
in the four-person relay team and soon all eyes will be on
you. The weight of a nation's pride will rest on your
fragile shoulders. In a few minutes' time the baton will be
in your hot little grabber and you'll be charging off in the
pursuit of immortal glory.

There it goes! The gun has sounded and the runners
are off down the straight. You wish it was all over
already—the suspense is chilling.

They round the first turn with your runner and another neck-and-neck. You hold your breath as the baton is
passed to number two in the team. Your crew are now

ahead by the slimmest of margins. You're biting your bottom lip so hard it starts to bleed a little. Frightening stuff this!

Suddenly you slip into automatic pilot—your body stiffens as you lean forward ready to take the next leg of the race. With arm outstretched behind you, you crane your neck to see where your team is placed. You're clearly in front now. All you have to do is hang on and, if you're lucky, you'll stretch the lead even further.

Then the baton is in *your* hand. Normally it's cold and steely but today you don't feel it at all, you just run. The crowd is on its feet and screaming down at you. You must be a good three metres in front by now—it's going better than you expected. In the flurry of excitement you look up and see the crowd of anxious faces glaring at you from the stands.

Ecstatic countrymen and women are furiously waving the homeland flag as you glide along on invisible wings. They're chanting your name in unison, thousands of voices all telling you you're a god. Your heart thumps harder, your pain is transformed into pure ecstasy and you take a moment to soak in the moment.

Then a terrifying realisation descends upon you. Your fans have stopped cheering. They're angry, they're jeering.

'God help me!' you scream inside. 'I've run too far!'

The fourth and final member of your team is twenty metres back but the baton is still in your hand. You've run right past your team-mate and the race is lost. Your legs give way under you and you're still unconscious when they drag you unceremoniously from the arena.

What happened? You fell in love with the moment, with your part of the race. For a fateful moment or two your forgot that you were just one member of a team, one part in a process.

Many modern Christians make that mistake. They fail to pass on the baton, to share what they've learned with younger Christians, to become fathers and mothers in the faith.

Needed Desperately: Fathers in the Faith

Fathers and mothers are in short supply in our society. Families are breaking up at a rapid rate and many younger people have never known the security of a real home. In the face of this onslaught against the family, the church can offer something which is not to be found elsewhere. Jesus said that if we give up fathers, mothers, brothers and sisters for His sake, we would receive one hundredfold in this life (Mark 10:30). What did He mean? He meant that the church itself would become like a family to us.

The church is not just yet another social club or networking organisation, it's a family. One of the greatest witnesses for the resurrection of Jesus is the 'familiness' of the church (Titus 2:1–8). Through the local church, Jesus offers us all the opportunity to learn from people who've blazed the trail before us.

When my father was growing up in church, young people were led to believe that if you couldn't lead public worship, preach, sing solo or run the Sunday school you didn't really have a 'ministry'. As a result we have a great many older people in our churches who feel they have nothing of value to contribute to the church of today. In fact they can offer us one of the most missed gifts in the church today—that of fathers and mothers in the faith.

So why am I writing all this for young leaders? Shouldn't I share this with some of the 'oldies' in the churches? I do, but I also believe that, as a Danish friend of mine has put it, 'If you're not a spiritual father by the time you're thirty, you'll never be one!'

Age has very little to do with it. Being a father or mother in the faith has to do with the inclination of your heart. Wisdom does not come simply because of age. The Bible doesn't say: 'The attainment of twenty-one years is the beginning of wisdom', or, 'Receiving your super-annuation payout is the beginning of wisdom.' It says, 'The fear of the Lord' is where wisdom begins (Ps. 111:10 KJV). In other words, wisdom comes from a heart attitude to God. It can be added to through life experience, but you can't get the true spiritual wisdom which is 'from above' (Jas. 3:17 KJV) simply by growing old. The basic prerequisite is a right heart towards God.

No matter what your age—as a person or as a Christian—you should right now be teaching others what you know (2 Tim. 2:2). You should be a spiritual father or mother to someone else.

Beware the Curse of Narcissus!

Ever heard the term: 'He's so goodlooking he's like a Greek god'? That's what people have always said about me. (I wish!)

Narcissus was a Greek guy who fitted the description to a T. He was more than handsome—he was beautiful. And didn't he know it. He was president, secretary and number-one ticket holder of his own fan club. Unbelievably vain.

Yet all the girls desired him. They broke out in a most unfeminine sweat whenever he glided by. They threw themselves at him, but did he succumb to their advances? No way, Horatio. He didn't even notice them.

It won't surprise you to know that Narcissus was one very lonely fella. He couldn't find anyone he thought worthy of his love. That is, not until one sunny afternoon as he walked by a lake. It was there he caught sight of his true love, the only one who could ever make him happy. He could hardly believe his luck—someone so beautiful so close to home. Why had they never met before?

He talked to the Beautiful One and the Beautiful One spoke back. They laughed together, they sang to each other, they shared intimate secrets. Hours went by as they sat drooling over each other.

Finally Narcissus could take the suspense no longer—he wanted a kiss. He waited for the right moment then leant forward for some lip-to-lip combat. Something strange happened—these lips were not wet, they were positively soggy! And when he looked down in surprise he found the object of his love had disappeared.

He waited a minute and, sure enough, his new friend returned. They reached out towards each other again and the same thing happened. It was heart-rending for Narcissus. Whenever he touched the Beautiful One, the Beautiful One vanished.

Days passed. Narcissus couldn't drag himself away. Weeks became months. The lovers didn't think about going home. They couldn't bare the thought of separation. Village girls often came to visit Narcissus. They tried everything to woo him away, but all was in vain. He was absolutely hooked, gone, beyond help.

They watched as his joy turned to morbid depression.

He could gaze at the Beautiful One but they could never touch. Eventually he lay there staring until he pined away. In death he was still gazing at the object of his love. Who was it that so besotted young Narcissus? It was himself—he fell in love with his own reflection in the lake!

We live in what is possibly the most narcissistic age in history. People are obsessed with looking after number one. I was flicking through my Bible the other day and came across *Psalm 23, Revised Yuppy Version*. It goes like this:

I am my own shepherd, I shall not want.
I lead myself down the road to personal success.
I restore my soul through positive thinking;
I guide myself in the paths of materialism for my own name's sake.
Even tho' I walk through the valley of the shadow of duty, I will fear no evil,
My Visa and American Express they comfort me!
I prepare a table of leisure before me in the presence of my responsibilities,
I anoint my head with gel;
My cup of Chateau Yaldara 1967 overflows.
Surely 'I Did It My Way' shall haunt me all the days of my life,
And I shall dwell in the house of loneliness cut off from God forever.

That kind of sums up the way many children of the 1990s go about the business of living. We're obsessed with our own reflections. Even Christians become selfish. How often do we give money to things which ultimately benefit ourselves and a few others (like church buildings and in-house church programmes)? How often do we pray for our needs alone?

A guy only four years younger than me once told me: 'Mal, you've been more like a father than a pastor to me.' I was very moved by that comment. I think it must be the most fantastic compliment anyone can pay a Christian leader, young or old.

Oh, I know what you're thinking: 'I've never had a father in the faith: no one has ever taken the trouble to really disciple me and train me for life and ministry. I don't have anyone like that to go to myself!' The failure of others to do their part is no excuse for our own neglect of God's call. This generation will have to do a better job of spiritual discipling than did the previous generation. So let's get on with it and stop complaining.

What does a father or mother in the faith look like? As you look through the qualities listed below, pray that God will develop these in your life.

Grace, You're Amazing!

When I was a kid, I always thought I'd like to meet Grace, whoever she was. I mean, everyone in church was always singing about how 'amazing' she was! Apparently she went around saving wretches (whatever they were) and helping lost and blind people. Some lady!

When I eventually discovered that the Grace in the song was not a person at all I was not disappointed in the slightest. In fact, grace seemed all the more amazing to me. What is grace? Grace is being shown mercy when you don't deserve it, which is what God has done for me. The hit songwriter of 1000 BC wrote that God deals with me not just in justice—according to what I legally deserve, but in mercy—giving me good things I could never earn (Ps. 51:1).

These days there's a lot of talk in the church about justice. That's good, but I think we should be primarily concerned with mercy which goes beyond giving people what they deserve and shares with them that for which they cannot pay. If we're merciful to others, we will automatically be just in the way we treat them.

God commands that I treat others the way He's treated me (Matt. 10:8). What does grace mean to a spiritual father or mother? It means changing in another person only what God wants changed. When we start discipling others for the Lord, it's easy to fall into the trap of making them in our own image. We want them to change to fit our tastes and our ideas. They should think as we do and like the same things as we like and agree with us on every issue. But that's not making them disciples, that's creating clones. There will be things about your disciple that you don't like but, if they're not forbidden in the law or principle of God's word, it's best not to demand their removal.

When I was first married, I learned something terrible about my good wife. (I hope she never reads this bit . . .) You'll be amazed to learn that—wait for it—my wife, good woman though she is, actually squeezed the toothpaste from the wrong end of the tube! I know, hard to believe in this day and age, isn't it?

I tried many times to change her habit. I explained that what she was doing was unhealthy, even unnatural. It was against the rule of ethics. It was even against God's law—it was immoral. But would she change? No way.

I needed a word from God on how to deal with an important issue like this so I prayed long and hard for my wife to change. Instead, God began to teach me a few lessons about grace. (Don't you ever wish God would only answer your prayers the way you think they should be answered?)

Finally I went to my wife and said: 'Look, I'm still not sure I like the way you handle the toothpaste tube. But, well, I can see that what you're doing isn't sinful in itself. So why don't you squeeze from your end and I'll squeeze from mine and we'll both get the job done together from different ends?'

Not only were my teeth brighter, but so was our marriage. Grace allows people to be unique. It does not expect them to be just like me in everything, even if I'm their spiritual mentor.

I Refuse to Change, So Don't Ask Me to . . .

OK, so we're about to have our first baby. Yes, it's kind of exciting, even a little bit overwhelming—I'm going to be a father. But I'm not going to get too carried away. After all, this baby has to learn who's boss around this house. Can't have a brat roaming all over the place. I've got it all worked out. I'll have it sleep in the garden shed, because there is NO way I'm losing any sleep for a baby. And I'll make sure it's locked safely away at five p.m. each day so that I can watch my favourite TV programmes in peace. Of course, it won't be allowed into the house again until nine o'clock next morning. That way I can enjoy an uninterrupted breakfast and be at work before the kid arrives.

Yes, I think it will all work out fine. If baby doesn't

like it, let him/her find somewhere else to live. I'm not changing my routine for anyone.

'Some father!' you say. I agree. Yet that's what some church people do when they see new people coming to Christ. They expect to go on with business as usual. New kids around the house always bring changes. Growth in the family demands change.

Hebrews 10:38 tells us that God's people live by faith. It goes on to say that He is not pleased with those who 'shrink back' in fear (NIV). Faith is an onward-moving thing. It doesn't spend its time reminiscing too much, or living in the past. It keeps adapting to new situations and needs. The one thing which keeps me praying and seeking God more than any other is the fear that one day I might be talking about the 'good ol' days'. I want to be involved with such great things in the future that I don't ever want to go back.

Tradition is not a bad thing. It's *traditionalism* which kills a move of the Holy Spirit. Traditionalism is refusing to hear a word from God unless it lines up with your tradition. Fathers and mothers in the faith are open to change. They refuse to be locked into one tradition. They refuse to say 'It's never been done this way before'. They are progressive, forward-looking people. They'll change—without compromising their standards—to adapt to growth.

I Could Be a Nice Guy, If Life Wasn't So Frustrating . . .

Frustration is a very annoying feeling. There's a lot in life to get frustrated about, too.

I was frustrated when I couldn't pass my test for my driver's licence. I bought a car and cleaned it up in readiness for the big day. It sat in the drive for months! I went for the practical driving test four times. It's OK for some people—they live in the country and simply have to drive twice around the football pitch and park between the goalposts. In my case, we had to negotiate big-city traffic.

Finally, through sheer persistence on my part—and sheer boredom on the part of the driving tester—I passed and was ready to take my second-hand car out for a run. I drove everywhere I could think of for two weeks. Sometimes I had nowhere to go, so I drove around the block a few thousand times. It felt good to be behind the wheel at last. But it was short-lived.

Two weeks after I passed the test, I was turning a corner and another driver pulled out in front of me. I hit him. I couldn't miss—*he was driving a bus!*

Life dishes out large doses of frustration. Even in our spiritual lives we can sometimes feel the tension building. When you've known the Lord for five years longer than the next guy, but he gets to run the home group, it's frustrating. When you pray and the ceiling above feels like it's made of solid kryptonite, that's frustrating.

I have some good friends who are well known in certain circles for their visionary status and powerful preaching ministries. Many times I've had to battle the frustration monster. As I've gazed in wonder (and envy) at the successes of others, I find myself feeling very frustrated at my own lack of results. Frustration has a way of turning us into threatened, mean individuals who have no time for anyone but ourselves. It cripples us as fathers or mothers in the faith.

The only way to overcome the threat of others'

199

success is to make those people your friends. You need to spend some time with them, learning what it is that drives them and letting some of their vision 'rub off' on you. When you're building relationships like this and personally investing in someone else's life, it's pretty hard to feel badly towards them. You want to protect them.

When frustration threatens to engulf you, there are two options open to you. Some people allow their frustration to make them cynical. A cynic is someone who smells the flowers then looks around for the funeral! I read about one cynic who carried an emergency ID card in his wallet which read: 'If I have an accident . . . I'm not surprised.'

The very first Psalm tells us to avoid sitting in the 'seat of the scornful' (Ps. 1:1 KJV). That's a true picture of the way cynics operate—they're always sitting down, never involved and forever criticising other people's efforts.

On the other hand, you can respond to frustration by allowing it to make you more sincere, more honest. When you own your frustration and avoid thrusting responsibility for it onto someone else, you can turn it into desperation. It's desperate people who reach out for something more than they presently possess and strain every muscle to achieve what God intended for them (Phil. 3:14).

I Answer to Nobody!

People these days can be very fickle in the keeping of commitments. The spirit of the age is one of 'no strings attached'. Like the Billy Horton character in the Bruce Springsteen song *Cautious Man*, many people tattoo on one hand the word 'love' and on the other hand the word 'fear'—they want to experience the joy of commitment but are afraid of being hurt.

There can be nothing more frustrating than trying to work with a disciple who shows no commitment. Many Christian leaders lament the fact that their people seem to show no attachment to the vision of their church or group, no ownership of the common dream. But people are not born (or even born again) committed, they learn commitment along the way.

In Luke 5 Jesus takes the disciples out into the deep water for a spot of fishing. Peter's not so sure this is a great idea since he's being burning the midnight oil in a vain attempt to snare a few sardines. Nevertheless he's willing to try anything for the sake of the business, so he takes Jesus out in the boat. They hook so many fish that they have to call in the coastguard to help drag them ashore. Fishburgers for a year!

What does Jesus say as they haul the catch ashore? 'I've helped you to catch fish, now you must help Me catch men.' Jesus showed commitment to these men before He ever asked it from them.

On another occasion Jesus demonstrated just how strong His commitments were. In Matthew 26:47–51 Judas comes to Him in the Garden of Gethsemane. It was here that Jesus had faced His bleakest hour prior to the cross. Here He agonised in prayer and asked that, if it were possible, the terrible cup of death should pass from His lips. In this place He bowed to the divine will and set His course towards Calvary.

As Judas comes forward to identify Jesus, the Lord looks him in the eye and says: 'Friend, do what you came to do.' The key word here is 'friend'. Long after Judas' commitment to Jesus has ceased, even when Judas is handing Him over to be crucified, Jesus still holds out the hand of friendship. That's real commitment.

The point here is that commitment is a learned response. From the time we are very young we develop skills of commitment only through seeing them demonstrated by others. People learn much more about commitment from what we do than from what we say, so we must model the level of commitment we want before we can expect to see it in our disciples.

That's why it is vital that every leader personally leads a life of accountability. Being accountable means giving someone the right to correct you and teach you how to be a true follower of Christ.

The very word 'disciple' speaks of learning. The Latin word *discere*, from which we get the word 'disciple', speaks of someone who is a student of another. A disciple is someone who is teachable.

I was saddened to hear a story behind the fall of a once great evangelist. This man who was reaching millions through his media ministry and preaching crusades, was asked by a management expert who in his organisation was able to say 'no' to him.

The preacher laughed. He called his assistant into the room and asked for the question to be repeated. The assistant laughed too. The whole idea of real accountability was a joke for them. A short time later the whole world was reading about the moral fall of this Christian world figure. Accountability is the key to safety.

The Bible demands three kinds of accountability from us. Firstly, we must live in accountability to God. Jesus told us not to fear man, who can destroy the body, but to fear God who can destroy the body and soul (Matt. 10:28).

It is to God that we will give ultimate account of our time on Spaceship Earth.

The Bible teaches accountability to our families. Married men and women will never be Christian leaders—people to whom others willingly give account—unless they know how to be accountable to their partners. Men must learn to be vulnerable with their wives. How many times do husbands hear their wives say: 'You never tell me anything!'? What they mean is that we seldom share more than our immediate wants. We don't let the guard down to expose our inner heart, our real feelings and dreams, with the women who love us.

Wives need to be loyal to their husbands. Loyalty is not unquestioning obedience. It is about doing what is in the other person's best interests even when it costs you something. Many men live under the weight of critical wives who will never accept even their partner's best effort to please them—nothing is good enough for them. Loyal wives try to encourage their husbands and compliment them on the good things they do. Even a rebuke can be encouraging when it is done with the other person's best interests at heart.

You might be thinking: 'Well, I'm off the hook in this family thing because I'm not married.' Wrong! You still have responsibility to honour your parents. 'Honour your father and mother' is the first command of God which has a promise attached, so we know it's important to God (Eph. 6:2). Of course, as we grow older we will not necessarily do everything our parents might tell us to do—maturity is about making one's own decisions in a responsible way. This may be especially true if our parents are not Christians. But we can still maintain the attitude of wanting to bless our parents, of respecting their opinions even if we don't always agree with them. That's a lifelong commitment.

We must also be personally accountable to the church. Ephesians 5:22 is a verse every husband enjoys reading: 'Wives, yield to your husbands, as you do to the Lord.' But the verse before is as important: 'Yield to obey each other because you respect Christ.' We are all to be in submission one to the other in the Body of Christ.

In practical terms I suppose this begins with being answerable to leaders in a local church setting. We should each willingly place ourselves under the authority of gifted leaders within our fellowship. The Bible teaches us that pastors and other leaders are Christ's gifts to His church and that they are given for the growth and development of each Christian (Eph. 4:12). If we fail to consider their direction and listen to their wisdom we are robbing ourselves of an opportunity to grow and learn.

Of course we cannot afford to give to any leader ultimate control over our decisions. Some have done this with tragic results. The local church is not meant to be a cult, complete with unquestioned demigod leadership. Ultimately we will give answer to God Himself and we should diligently seek God's mind for direction in all our decisions. In good churches, however, the oversight will be encouraging us to do just that. They will not insist on being the only voice we will hear and will teach us how to hear from God for ourselves.

If you have never sat down for a real 'heart-to-heart' with your pastor, now would be a good time to try it. You will benefit from just sharing your dreams with a key leader and letting him or her become part of your development. But you must be willing to listen to wisdom or correction.

Now when the Bible speaks about submission to the church it is not simply referring to the leadership. The people who make up the church also provide covering for us.

This kind of accountability has nothing to do with just going to church each week. In practical terms it is not really possible to be accountable to large numbers of people. Real accountability begins when we gather around ourselves a small group of three or four peers with whom we meet every week or so for prayer and sharing. This kind of fellowship group provides an avenue for practical accountability. It might be easy to hide in a crowd on Sunday, but it's difficult amidst a group of friends who know us well.

Nobody should be above correction. Every one of us needs someone who can say 'no' to us. You cannot be a father or mother in the faith without a commitment to a local body of believers. People who are forever 'church-hopping', moving from group to group, are setting themselves up for a fall. They are afraid to pay the price of real accountability and are missing the safety of fellowship.

We will always reproduce after our own kind and unteachable leaders produce unteachable disciples.

Will the Real You Please Stand Up?

Imagine that you were trying to establish yourself as a world leader. Picture yourself gathering around you a group of assistants, men whom you want to convince of your special leadership abilities. You want to train these

205

guys to take your ideas, your message, to the world. You want them to serve you without question because they've seen you in action and believe that you are the only hope for the planet.

Outside your home town you've been working some pretty amazing miracles. Unfortunately, whenever you come home people treat you like furniture. Do you bring your devoted followers into your home, where everyone takes you for granted? Are you going to endanger all your grandiose plans by letting your unbelieving brothers weaken the faith of your followers? Hardly. You'll work hard to keep cynical family members and impressionable disciples as far away from each other as possible.

That's not what Jesus did when faced with this situation. Rather than hide from dissension, He actually exposed His disciples to differences of opinion. In John 2:12 we are told that on occasion He travelled with both His disciples and His family members in one group.

We don't know what transpired on that ministry trip to Capernaum, but you can imagine Jesus' brothers, who were not believers at this time (John 7:5), making cynical remarks about His claims to Messiahship within clear hearing range of Peter and the boys. Cynics are like that: they can't resist a chance to spread their negative views.

But Jesus didn't need to put a show on for His disciples, so He was not afraid to have them see all of this. He was so real, so secure that nothing could dent His confidence in His call. He was the same Jesus at home with the cynics as He was preaching to thousands of believers.

Some leaders turn their disciples into great archaeologists. Their followers learn to dig deep to find the real leader underneath all the masks and phoney images.

Unfortunately, archaeologists never really know the people whose stories they uncover. It's sad that so many leaders do not let people get close enough to know them.

Fathers and mothers in the faith are not afraid to be themselves. They don't freak out if one of their disciples discovers a weakness in them, or questions their wisdom. They are cool in the face of criticism because they know who has called them and they are completely aware of their strengths and their weaknesses. Paranoid, defensive leaders always produce insecure people.

I once heard Dr Tony Campolo say that he doesn't really care too much what people think of his message or his personality, because he knows that Jesus thinks he's great! That's a secure leader, and one who's easy to like.

Fathers and mothers in the faith are not threatened if their disciples learn something from someone else either.

Picture this: Johnny is five years old. He's just started school and he feels quite proud of his new status as a student. He arrives home one afternoon and races over to his father. 'Daddy,' he says, grinning proudly from ear to ear, 'Guess what! I learned about how to cross the road today!'

Dad throws down his paper in disgust. 'How dare you learn to cross the road! Did I teach you that? No! I'll decide when you should learn that. Now go away and forget what they told you. We'll get to it when I'm good and ready.'

Is this guy insecure or what?! He's not a true father, because a true father wouldn't care where you learned the truth—he'd simply rejoice that you had heard it.

That was Jesus' way. His disciples came to Him one day complaining because someone was baptising people in

His name. 'Why don't we get down there and shut this guy up?' they mumbled. 'Who does he think he is, muscling in on our turf?'

What was Jesus' response? 'Hey, guys, relax! Whoever's not against us is for us. If they're preaching God's truth, they're on our team' (Mark 9:40).

Jesus was quite happy for people to receive blessing from the ministries of others. He's secure in His call and has the best interests of the people at heart. He doesn't mind who is preaching His name, so long as people are being led to the Kingdom of God.

That's what secure leaders, real disciple-makers, are like. They will gladly expose their followers to other ministries which compliment their own. They'll try to ensure that everyone is given a well-rounded schooling in the faith.

Get Organised!

Here's a little truth to store away in memory banks: *no one follows a slob!* If you lead a sloppy, disorganised life, don't expect people to relate to you for long. Effective fathers in the faith know how to make people feel secure. They demonstrate discipline in the way they manage their own affairs.

Being organised means knowing what your priorities are and sticking to them. Unfortunately none of us can save the world all on our own—none of us have the gifts necessary to do it, nor the time and energy. Even Jesus knew His human limitations. He learned how to maximise His time and energy through careful, prayerful organisation of His time.

Reinhard Bonnke is one of the best-known healing evangelists in the world today. His crusades in poor African nations attract crowds numbering hundreds of thousands.

I preached at a conference with him in Kassell, Germany and was very interested in speaking with him about his success. 'You've been a great example to many younger men and women—a real testimony of what faith can do,' I said. 'Well, I guess I'm just a single-minded man,' he replied. No fuss, no fanfare, just a simple conviction and a burning passion for people.

Single-mindedness would have to be one of the most underrated qualities a Christian leader can possess. Many young leaders have never thought about what their priorities should be. They live off the dreams of others and settle for second best.

According to the book of James, a person who has no clearly defined priorities is insecure and unstable in everything he or she does (Jas. 1:8).

My priorities may not be yours

The Bible clearly teaches that you and I will differ in our views on certain issues and neither of us will be better than the other (1 Cor. 8:7–12), 10:25–29). There are issues on which we must refer judgement to our individual consciences. In some respects what is good for you is not necessarily good for me!

So it's no good for you to be following my priorities exactly. You must seek God for your own path to your prize in Christ. Sure, we're all saved by the same means and filled with the same Spirit, but each of us is given a different part to play in God's overall scheme.

It's always easier to follow someone else's path rather

than hack out your own— eating the fruit is easier than sowing the seed—which explains why so many young leaders do just that. They settle for second best. They accept hand-me-downs when they could have tailor-made priorities.

Priorities change

Change is never comfortable. Frankly, it can be a real drag at times. Just when you think you've got things all worked out, something new happens and destroys the plot.

God works through change. He changes the scenery on us every so often so that we become vulnerable again. God relates to the spirit of brokenness because it is open to new growth (Ps. 51:17).

We must constantly be reviewing our priorities, opening the windows of our dreams for the fresh breeze of the Spirit to blow and rearrange them as He wishes. It's a good idea actually to set time aside for this every day. Our prayer and Bible reading time should feature space for just sitting still, reflecting on where we've come from and where we're going.

It's also a good idea to make special appointments with the Holy Spirit—to get away for a retreat once or twice per year. Just pack up and go and hide away for a couple of days of prayer and fellowship with the Boss. Jesus often did this kind of thing.

Not too long ago I was leading a tour of around thirty people through Israel. Most had never been before and were eager to follow in the footsteps of Jesus. I asked one guy what he'd got out of the trip.

'I've learned that Jesus really liked mountains!' he replied. It was a great observation—Jesus did spend large amounts of time away from the crowds hearing from God on the steep hills around Galilee and Jerusalem. It was here that the Father shaped His priorities.

I remember the first time I recorded a solo studio album. We spent around $10,000 dollars on it—a lot of money for an Aussie Christian album in the early 1980s. The time in the studio was fun and the final product was good, but the part of the project from which came the fondest memories was the prayer retreat which went before it.

The whole scheme was birthed in my spirit during a lone prayer retreat. I just rented a house by a beach and, in the middle of winter, paced the sands seeking God for a direction, a priority for my music. Some of the songs were written on those sand-swept beaches. The title for the album came to me there as did the basic sleeve design. I've had similar 'mountain-top' experiences at other times and I've been inspired to develop and move on. If it was good enough for Jesus, it's good enough for us.

Having priorities does not make you selfish

Some leaders mistake having solid priorities for being myopic. They can only see and appreciate whatever it is they're doing—they can't get interested in anyone else's vision.

God only invests His dreams in those who invest in the dreams of others. You can be single-minded and at the same time encourage the gifts and ministries of fellow Christians. In fact, no worthwhile goal is ever achieved by one person acting on their own. God has made us dependent on each other by limiting the gifts each person possesses.

Our priorities must be flexible enough to be shaped around the ideas and strengths of fellow dreamers.

Vision precedes provision

There's one line I've heard a few too many times: 'I'm just waiting for God to prosper me so that I can give generously to the Kingdom of God.'

I ask myself: if you don't give when you have little, what makes you think you'll be more liberal when you have much? This is a wrong attitude. The Bible says more about provision than prosperity. What is prosperity? Basically it is having enough to accomplish a Godly vision.

Hebrews 13:20–21 sums up the Bible's teaching on the subject: 'I pray that the God of peace will give you every good thing you need so you can do what he wants.'

The very word provision is made up of two parts: 'pro' meaning 'for', and 'vision'. Provision comes *for* vision. God's provision comes in response to vision, not in anticipation of it. If you have no priorities mapped out by faith, don't expect God to bring in the wherewithal to make something happen. Vision comes first, then provision.

Priorities are balanced

Ever met a person who does not know how to relax? You know, a workaholic, someone who doesn't know how to stop. Of course there are others who are afraid to start—they are workaphobics. Both have problems: their priorities are not balanced.

The ministry of Jesus Christ is a constant balancing act, a commitment to many responsibilities at once. You cannot neglect your family for the ministry and you can't deny your ministry to spend all your time at home with the family.

One of the biggest traps leaders can fall into is that of never being able to say 'no' to anything. They feel they have to be in everything all the time. Elton Trueblood (he's a writer, not a heavy metal musician) made this comment: 'A public man, though he is available at many times, must learn to hide. For if he does not learn to hide he will not be worth anything when he is available.' Good one, Elton!

There are many time-wasters in the ministry. There are the people who have one foot nailed to the floor. You know the kind: they come to you for counselling every week with the same old problem. They know how to solve it, but they won't try. Jesus said we should shake the dust off our Reeboks and move on to others who will do what is required (Matt. 10:14).

Then there are those who have one ear welded to the phone. They call at all odd hours, pleading with you to come and help them, claiming that you're the only one who cares and can solve the problem. Unfortunately, you're not the Messiah, so don't feel you have to act like one. Do your best, but don't let people manipulate you by tickling your ego.

Learn to say 'no' when necessary. It's the only way to keep your sanity.

Fathers and mothers in the faith are people of clear priorities. Jesus could say 'Follow Me' with a conviction which made men drop everything and follow—because His priorities were clear.

Our priorities will be shaped largely by the needs around us and our particular gifts. Ministry is about responding both to the needs of people and to the call of God. Unless we constantly reappraise our priorities in prayer, we might find ourselves spending our energies on fruitless exercises. On the other hand, if we never take time to identify with practical needs around us, our praying will have little effect.

We have multitudes of preachers in the modern church and many Christian music artists, but we suffer a constant and chronic lack of fathers and mothers in the faith. We still have a few too many Christian 'superstars' and not nearly enough 'super-servants'.

A radical commitment to personally discipling younger people can be taxing—emotionally, spiritually and even financially—but if the church's influence in society is to grow and not diminish in the coming years, it's this kind of commitment we need to see. Those of us who've had too few fathers must now seek to become fathers to the next generation.

Recommended Reading

Great Christians of the Past

Arnot, Anne, *The Secret Country of C. S. Lewis*, Lakeland (Marshall, Morgan and Scott), 1983.

Berry, W. Grinton, *Fox's Book of Martyrs*, Baker Book House, 1978.

Broomhall, Marshall, *The Man Who Believed God . . . The Story of Hudson Taylor*, China Inland Mission Overseas Missionary Fellowship, 1929.

Davey, Cyril, *The Glory Man . . . A New Biography of Billy Bray*, Hodder & Stoughton, 1979.

Dennis, Lane T. (ed.), *The Letters of Francis Schaeffer*, Kingsway Publications, 1985.

Douglas, W. M., *Andrew Murray and His Message*, Baker Book House, 1981.

Ellis, William T., *Billy Sunday, the Man and His Message*, Moody Press, 1959.

Frodsham, Stanley Howard, *Smith Wigglesworth, Apostle of Faith*, Gospel Publishing House, 1948.

Grubb, Norman, *Rees Howells, Intercessor*, Lutterworth Press, 1976.

Grubb, Norman, *C. T. Studd*, Lutterworth Press, 1970.

Kennedy, Neil L., *Dream Your Way to Success* (authorised biography of Dr Yonggi Cho), Logos International, 1980.

Lawrence, Carl, *The Church in China, How it Survives and Prospers under Communism,* Bethany House, 1985.

Pratney, Winkey, *Revival,* Whitaker House, 1983.

Skinner, Tom, *Black and Free,* Paternoster Press, 1968.

Steer, Roger, *George Muller, Delighted in God,* Hodder & Stoughton, 1981.

Wessel, Helen (ed.), *The Autobiography of Charles G. Finney* (condensed), Bethany Fellowship Inc., 1977.

Whitaker, Colin, *Seven Pentecostal Pioneers,* Marshall Pickering, 1983.

For bookings and information on other materials

Write to:

Mal Fletcher Ministries
PO Box 83
Moorabbin 3189
Victoria
Australia

STREETS OF PAIN

Bill Wilson

. . . a story of hope for an abandoned generation

Do these sound like the kids in your Sunday School?

Patrick's father is serving jail time for first degree murder.
Isabel's mother stays in a mental institution because of addiction to drugs.
Kim has permanent scars on her forehead because of a beating at the age of five.

These are the members of Metro Church, a congregation of eleven thousand children located in the crumbling heart of Brooklyn, New York. A determined young man named Bill Wilson founded the church in 1980. Today, each week, more then fifty full-time staff members and two hundred volunteers between them visit each child who comes to the Metro Sunday School. The ministry to children has also spawned a one-thousand-member adult congregation.

The risk is great in the inner city. Week after week Wilson and his staff battle everything from rats to fatigue, from muggings to lice. This fast-paced, moving account will give you a fresh perspective on the problems of the inner city and the children who live there. It will also give you exciting, new ideas on what it takes to reach the children who need Jesus in your own city.

Catalogue Number YB 9607   £4.25

DESPERATELY SEEKING ADVICE

Sue Ritter

Calling All Young People!

Are you looking for answers to your problems? Do you keep getting fobbed off by people who just don't understand? Worry not, Sue Ritter **does** understand. Working in schools and youth evangelism, Sue helps you on tricky questions like:

When you become a Christian, how do you:

- Tell your friends?
- Cope when your non-Christian family makes life difficult for you?
- Manage to keep up with your old friends as well as your Christian friends without losing touch?
- Behave? Do you have to dress differently i.e. boringly or sensibly?
- 'Give everything to God'?
- Pray when you can't?
- Read the Bible when it doesn't seem to make sense?

Calling All Youth Leaders!

Haven't you always wanted to say . . . 'Here read this, it tells you what you need to know'? Well, this book has been created especially for you!

Catalogue Number YB 9596   £3.99

101 DYNAMIC IDEAS – FOR YOUR YOUTH GROUP

Andy Back

Tired of all those worn-out games and the dull routine of your youth group? Tired of reading Christian books with no jokes in them? Tired of owning £3.99? Then this is the book for you!

A high-speed ride through sports, competitions, games, workshops, events, parents' evenings, stayovers, crafts, wide games, daftness, and leadership principles.

There is little room for the faint-hearted in youth work, but this book proves that there's loads of room for the light-hearted and dedicated. Begone, drabness! Come on down, fun, excitement, adventure and amazing things!

Catalogue Number YB 9702   £3.99

ACTS OF GOD

Andy Back

Peter, Paul and the apostles battled against almost impossible odds, preaching the gospel to a world which didn't want to hear. A story of baskets, swords, soldiers, salvation, whips, jails, prayer meetings, chariots, church-planting, visions and shipwreck.

Put yourself in Paul and Peter's shoes! Sing as you're thrown into jail for the umpteenth time! Trust God for strength as you're run out of town by an angry mob! Stand up and preach the good news of the Lord Jesus Christ!

The drama of the book of the Acts of the Apostles unfolds in modern language, making these true stories as fresh as the day they were written.

Catalogue Number YB 9701   £2.25

DAN THE MAN

Andy Back

Daniel and his three friends remain obedient to the Lord as they face trials and trouble in a foreign land! A story of sand, lions, fires, idols, kings, madness, faith, visions, vegetables, graffiti and godliness.

Be like Daniel! Feel the hot breath of the lions against the back of your neck! Trust God to help you as the King makes extraordinary and unreasonable demands! Be amazed and excited at what God is doing as you face strange and bewildering beasts!

The drama of the book of Daniel unfolds in modern language, making these true stories as fresh as the day they were written.

Catalogue Number YB 9700   £2.25

NO COMPROMISE

Melody Green & David Hazard

Even if you've never heard Keith Green's songs, it's time to hear the message of his life.

He fought against compromised beliefs selling out for popularity, and the dust of religious institutions. His challenge raised up leaders from ordinary young men and women. Keith was a champion to some. A lightning rod of controversy to others. Keith's life story, his music and the never-before-published journal sections in *No Compromise* are a road map to where he was headed spiritually. Hailed as a prophet by many, he often struggled painfully to live up to his own strong declarations.

And just when Keith found a new secret—one that set him free inside—he was taken from us. He was only 28.

Keith's spiritual search, and what he learned at that final turn in the path, had much more to say to us. It will set your feet on higher ground.

No one knew Keith better than the woman who shared his life and mission—his wife, Melody.

In July, 1982, when Keith was killed in a tragic plane crash along with two of their children—Josiah, 3 and Bethany, 2—Melody was left with one-year-old Rebekah. She was also pregnant with her fourth child, Rachel. And she inherited Keith's musical legacy of published and unpublished songs and his private journals.

Catalogue Number YB 9318   £5.99

A NEW CREATION
J. John

Have you ever been out of God's plan for a while?
Given up praying? Put yourself down? Felt
spiritually depressed? Or have you consciously hurt
God and don't know how to approach Him? Was
your first experience with Christ totally incredible?
And are you now struggling to live the Christian life?

J. John, in his own dynamic and friendly style of
communicating, has picked up on an assortment of
spiritual problems and suggests the main cause is
that your Christian life is being led your way, but in
Christ you are *a new creation* (2 Corinthians 5:17),
and therefore should be following God's way.

J. John shows you how the old self has gone and the
new needs to discover and rediscover God's path—
so that you can lead a more consistent and wholly
satisfied Christian life.

Catalogue Number YB 9558   £3.99